The Ultimate Massage Marketing and Business Book

Sabrina Tonneson

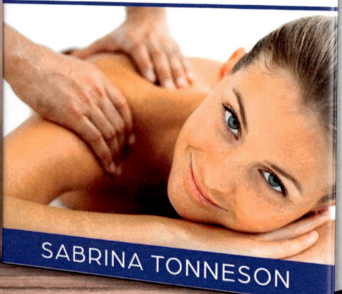

© 2018 Sabrina Tonneson

All rights reserved. No portion of this book may be reproduced in any form without permission from the publisher, except as permitted by U.S. copyright law.

For permissions contact: SabrinaTonneson@gmail.com

Author's website www.MassageMarketing101.com

Dedicated to Moriah and Andre

Table of Contents

Massage Marketing - Boost Profits - Book 1 11

Introduction 13

Why Create A Business Menu? 16

Pricing Mistakes 19

Designing Your Menu - Different Types Of Consumers 21

Design Your Menu - Spa Packages 23

Design Your Menu - First Time Customers 26

Design Your Menu - Wellness Programs Or Membership Programs 30

Design Your Menu - How To Create A Membership Contract 34

Design Your Menu - Massage Therapy Enhancements 37

Design Your Menu - Birthday Offers 41

Design Your Menu - Referrals 43

Design Your Menu - Loyalty Reward Program 46

Financial Goals 48

Research And Raising Prices 52

Sample Menu Plan 54

Pricing And Menu Worksheet 59

Success Stories 63

Massage Marketing - Book 2 67
Introduction 69
Grow Your Business Quickly 71
#1 Tip For Success 73
Create The Ambiance - Lighting 77
Create The Ambiance - Eye Pillow 78
Create The Ambiance - Scents 79
Create The Ambiance - Layout And Design 82
Create The Ambiance - Massage Table 83
Create The Ambiance - Neck Pillow 85
The Art Of Hot Towels 86
Learning New Techniques 88
Get Raving Fans With Hot Stones 90
Beverages And Snacks 92
Different Types Of Packages 93
Packages Names And Descriptions 96

Add On The Serenity - Book 3 103
Introduction 105
Create Your Upgrade List 107
Face & Scalp Upgrades 109
Body And Feet Upgrades 113
Seasonal & Promotional Upgrades 116
Outside The Box Upgrades 119
Upgrade Description And Pricing 123

Selling Upgrades 126
Marketing Upgrades To New Clients.. 129

Ultimate Gift Card Sales & Marketing Secrets - Book 4 131
Introduction 133
Secret #1 - Avoid Underpricing 134
Secret #2 - Year-Round Sales... 137
Secret #3 - Terms 139
Secret #4 - The Magic Of Buy 1, Get 1 144
Secret #5 – Semi-Annual Gift Card Campaign 149
Double Your Holiday Gift Card Sales 153
Sell More Gift Certificates Without Under Pricing....................153
Bonus Book 153
Black Friday Deals.. 155
Offer A Variety Of Packages... 159
Strategic Ways To Get New Customers................................... 162
Sell Gift Certificates Online.. 166
Sell More Gift Cards At Your Business Location 168
25 Countdown Days - Social Media Engagement 170

Massage Marketing - Sorry We're Booked - Book 5 173
Introduction 175
Book Your Slow Days... 178
Showcase Your Services With A Photo Testimony 184
Texting Promotions 186

Get Others To Promote You 188
Teach A Class 190
The Power Of "Thank You" 192
Creating Promotional Offers 193
Last Minute Deals 196
Loyalty Reward Program 198
Promotional Referral 200
Rebooking Offers 203
Thanks, But No Thanks 205

Massage Therapy Enhancements - Book 6 207
Introduction 209
Basalt Hot Stone Massage 211
Bamboo Massage 213
Jade Roller Face Massage 216
Himalayan Salt Stone Massage Therapy 218
Massage Cupping 221
Kansa Wand 223
Massage Blading 225
References 227
Marble Cold Stone Massage 228
Hot Stone Foot Massage 230
Dry Brushing 232
Sugar Scrubs 234
Thai Herbal Massage Balls 236

Non-Professionals - At Home Massage Tips 238
Professionals - Tips 241

Massage Marketing - Boost Profits

Book 1

Sabrina Tonneson

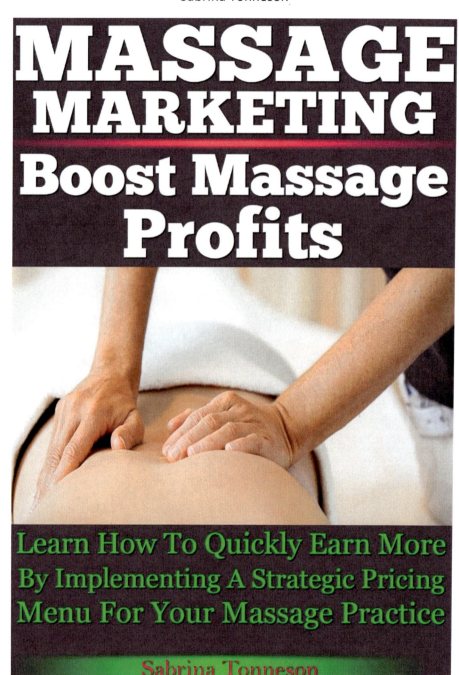

Introduction

Most massage therapists embark on their careers with one fundamental motivation, a deep desire to help and heal others with massage therapy.

They plough their heart, soul, muscle and sinew into their careers and customers, yet they don't always harvest an income reflecting all they've invested in their business. Many of them are burdened with being overworked and underpaid.

Even though you are drawn to a deeper calling, the vocation of healing hands, you can't very well deposit feelings of Zen and inner peace at the bank.

You may be wondering; how can you hang a price tag on big heartedness? Healing compassion can't be quantified in dollars and cents, can it?

Even with all my considerable experience, I can't do that. What I can do, though, is help you shake up your business, making it more productive, efficient and lucrative.

Indeed, the purpose of this book is to help you, as a massage therapist, perceive what you do as a legitimate business. With the application of the principles detailed in this book, you can achieve a more favorable work-to-income balance, making your massage therapy as rewarding for you as it is for your clients.

This book asks and answers some important questions. How do

you select prices for your massage practice? Why is undercharging a mistake? How can a business leverage more revenue with proper pricing? Why is your menu one of the most important pieces of your marketing? How does implementing a menu grow your business?

It's something that's easy to overlook, but a strategic menu is the most effective marketing maneuver of any massage practice.

This book will show you how to construct a menu that is a painless path to boosting profits without additional investments of time and money. Inside this book, you'll find step-by-step instructions for a profit-boosting business menu.

With a menu in hand, you can determine the best pricing. This is a critical step because pricing your services appropriately allows you to earn more while working less.

In here, you'll find worksheets and formulas to assist in the design and creation of your massage therapy services.

This book will teach you how to accelerate business growth by offering a variety of services.

Failing to charge properly for your work is like walking away from money. A menu detailing your services is a cost-free way to market your business, lure new customers and lock in all important repeat clients.

Every massage practice can benefit from this marketing tool, regardless of the size of your business.

My name is Sabrina Tonneson and I have over two decades of massage therapy experience. My practice had its humble beginnings in my home. Working from home, though, was more complicated than I had pictured in my head! Soon enough, I transplanted my fledgling operation to a rented room. Success quickly beckoned, so I leased my own space and expanded the business by hiring staff.

Over the years of owning and managing a massage therapy practice, I've discovered through trial and error, how to pilot a successful enterprise. Admittedly, one of my greatest challenges was mental fatigue.

At one point, my drive and enthusiasm cooled to crippling ennui. In addition to demotivation, burnout became a steady, unwelcome companion. I needed some kick-in-the-butt stimulation, and that came in the way of new services, new techniques and new marketing approaches.

My passion is creating business success. I've been mentoring individual businesses and companies for over 10 years.

Take it from me, running your own business means you need to be like an octopus, with many tentacles efficiently conducting different functions. I can help you cut an easy path to success.

It's my mission to guide massage therapists to achieve balance and distil appreciation and healthy compensation from hard work.

This book is dedicated to all of you with selfless hearts, nurturing souls, and sainted hands. If you follow the simple formulas and effective marketing tools contained in this book, you'll be assured of greater financial rewards for your talents.

Why Create A Business Menu?

Proper pricing and a strategic menu are oxygen to any service-oriented business.

A fatal flaw of many massage therapists is the one service (massage therapy) one flat rate' mindset. That is a proven recipe for short-changing yourself. Even as a solo entrepreneur, a solid menu will transform your business. You need to design an effective menu to function as a blueprint for your pricing structure.

Before we delve into pricing, let's first focus on the importance of a menu. Massage therapy clients come from all walks of life. An understanding of your client demographics is the foundation of a services menu that checks every box in your client pool.

I'm going to describe some of the typical massage therapy clients coming across your table. Try to think of them like exotic birds.

There's the "I need to get a massage NOW!" customer. For this species of client, cost is of little consequence. The customer who needs a massage like an asthmatic needs an inhaler is willing to pay extra if you extend your hours to fit them in. Availability, not price, is their priority.

Then there's the "I'll shop around for a better deal" customer. This species is identified by their behavioral patterns, popping up when you dangle specials or low prices out there. They're most abundant during the sale season and are willing to schedule early in the morning or late in the evening. This customer's priority is snagging a bargain.

Another type of customer is the regular. This client is already sold on the benefits of a weekly or monthly massage. This particular species is searching for a life- mate, a massage therapist with the desired skill set. In the massage client world, this customer is, perhaps, the most sought-after species of them all. Stay with me on the exotic birds' analogy here!

And, of course, you have the high roller client. This peacock-like customer, for whom money is no object, is accustomed to being pampered. This species is known for strutting about and doing things like scheduling your deluxe packages. They want the best you can offer, while they drift off in a gentle current of serenity conjured by your spellbinding hands. That's the spare- no expense client.

Those are just a few of the customers that massage therapists encounter. Most businesses cater to a varied clientele so their menus and prices reflect this diversity.

Hotels are an excellent example of this pricing strategy. They apply higher nightly rates during peak periods and modest rates when demand slows. This follows the natural cycles of tourism seasons.

As a budget-conscious traveler, you probably vacation during the low season. If you are a high-end consumer, though, you'd likely book the most luxurious hotel suite, peak season or not. Similarly, restaurants have early bird dinner specials or happy hour specials. Such deals target the budget consumer willing to patronize their business during periods of slowed diner traffic.

Smart marketers create a variety of items on their menu. Your massage or service can benefit from the same marketing strategy.

If you can get past the thinking that you offer one basic item at a flat rate, you'll harness a huge marketing advantage and grow your practice double-time! You can attract a variety of customers with a menu designed to cater to their needs, wants and budgets.

Keep in mind, you can continue to massage that long-term goal of a specialization that most fits your preferences. A varied menu can help grow your practice at a faster pace, getting you closer to your ultimate business objectives. As appointments become filled and your customer base expands, you can adjust your marketing approach. Dropping services from your menu is always an option. You are the creator of your business, the captain of your destiny.

Pricing Mistakes

So, I've already identified the 'one service, one price' pitfall common to many massage therapists. These businesses are too hasty in fixing their prices. Insufficient thought and strategy have gone into the process. Sometimes a business practitioner assumes if they charge the going rate in their area, then that's good enough.

Pricing, though, should be practiced as a function of marketing. Often, businesses start out hot and heavy, realizing shortly afterwards that their prices are too low. There you are with marketing and business materials already printed and the figures are depressingly off base. That can put you in a very tight spot. Penciling in new prices early in the life of a business can douse customers' interest. Instead of alienating customers, or flushing dollars down the tubes on printed materials, put in some time on research. Read this book and do the worksheets.

Have you heard the story of the two tree cutters, Tom and Larry? Every day Tom and Larry went to the woods to cut dead branches and fell dead trees. Larry spent several hours every day pruning trees. His neighbor, Tom, spent less time on the same task. One day Larry asked Tom how he manages to finish his tasks so quickly. Tom responded, "I prepare the saw in advance." Larry jumped in, exclaiming, "I don't have time to waste on preparing my saw!" Tom smiled and gently said, "Preparing the saw sharpens the blade. A sharp blade allows me to cut easily and effectively. A sharp blade allows me to finish quickly."

So, do you sharpen your blades before you start sawing your customers? Wait, I've taken the analogy a bit too far! Ask yourself: do you sharpen up on your marketing before getting out there? This simple story illustrates the value of preparation. Some call it working smart versus working hard.

It makes more sense to do your research and fashion strategies before racing off to promote your services. Your menu and pricing constitute strategic business-building tools. It's all about getting repeat business and attracting new customers.

Another classic mistake is underestimating the time it takes to build a customer base. I've witnessed this problem time and again. Business is slower than anticipated. I know, I'll drop my prices! That should drum up more appointments!

Flat rate, price drop - every day, business flop. Here's how the problem becomes intractable. That strategy only appeals to customers trawling for discounts and special offers. If you run flat rate specials every week, before you know it, you've dug yourself into a discount hole. The clients who respond to that sort of marketing will expect nothing less.

When you understand that your services attract a variety of customers, you can target them in different ways. Consequently, your business will function efficiently at different price ranges, all while promoting the massage services that most appeal to you.

Designing Your Menu - Different Types of Consumers

First things first, draw up a list of the categories of services you can offer. Mind you, this is the research phase, nothing's set in stone.

This is just the creative process. Put your brain into overdrive and see if you can come up with some more ideas that would fit your business.

New customers, Spa package customers, Wellness Program customers, Membership customers, Coupon customers, Urgent scheduling,

Best deal customers, Celebration customers,

Specialty services, and Luxury packages

You want to identify these customers because you should market them differently. Resist the instinct to lump all advertising in one category.

For example, the price of a 60-minute massage is $75.00. New customer, same price.

Monthly customers, same price.

Slow season, same price.

If your busiest day of the week is Saturday, don't offer promotions on Saturdays. Saturday should be the day you bring in the most money. Keep your discounts for your slow days.

Offering a variety of services allows you to target clients at different price points. It is smart marketing. Jump on this insight to build a successful, sustainable business.

Design Your Menu - Spa Packages

Why offer spa packages?

Depending on the services you include, you can earn more money within the same time period. Spa packages allow you to charge more for extra services and products.

Hot stone massage is an in-demand moneymaker. It's all about adding value to the same service.

There will be an initial investment to buy products for these value-added services. On the upside, they can be used repeatedly, with no further out-of-pocket expenses. The 60-minute session doesn't take any longer, you're just charging more for the allotted time on account of the enhanced service.

You can also allocate money to create luxury packages. Keep in mind, decadent, organic massage oils, body scrubs, polishes, and butter creams will be a bigger investment per session because those inputs aren't reusable. However, you can still make more money on the spa packages as the cost of those inputs will always be less than the price of the service. The use of such products gives you the flexibility to infuse your menu with more luxury offerings.

Always be mindful of the wording used to create your packages. Look at the difference between these three services.

- 60 minute massage $75.00

- 60 minute massage with hot stones $95.00

Relaxation Package

Enjoy a 60-minute customized massage. Your massage package includes deep relaxing hot stones and a hot towel peppermint foot treatment. Melt your stress away with this massage package. Regular price $99.00 On Sale $79.00

If you were a potential customer mulling over these three options, which one would appeal to you? The package that offers more value attracts customers. The package that allows the customer to imagine the experience will attract more business.

Put your spa packages at higher prices. The higher price reflects the additional value and products included in the package. Customers want to feel they are getting good value for their dollars.

Higher prices also allow the business to adjust the sale price as business picks up. As your appointment book fills up, your sale prices change. Sale prices can increase without having to change your original menu price.

If your services start out at a higher price point, it allows your business to make more money without updating printed material or telling customers your prices are going up.

You can also promote the services that most tickle your fancy. If Lavender Infusion Massage is your thing, then list that spa package on sale and keep the other spa packages at regular price.

Another benefit of higher priced spa package is gratuity. Many clients do a flat rate percentage. Higher prices will yield higher tips.

For more information on how to create spa packages please read my book:

Massage Marketing - Don't Leave Money On The Table Earn more money with an infusion of creative services to reel in more clients. www.MassageMarketing101.com

Design Your Menu - First Time Customers

Promotions are an effective way to reel in first timers. You can offer a special without applying a discount to every customer.

This new customer incentive can be fluid. You have the freedom to change the offer monthly. If there are several openings available, sweeten the new customer offer. If you are almost fully booked, fix the offer at a smaller discount. If you are able to access your website editing and online scheduling, it's easy to update the promotion of your new customer offer.

One great way to add value to a first-time client is with the inclusion of some of the tools or products that cost you little or nothing.

For example, if you've purchased hot stones, throw those in on the deal. This will amp up the value without an additional cost to you. If you have extra products you want to use, include those as well.

You may have a half-gallon of mango butter or peppermint sugar scrub products and they are approaching their expiration date. Create a package with a mango butter hydrating hand & foot treatment or peppermint sugar scrub treatment. That's an irresistible lure.

Set up a page on your website directed at new customers. Give potential new clients some insight into what they can expect when they visit your practice. If you're not keen on hard membership sales, include that information. Highlight your specialties. If you don't deduct 10 minutes for changing, share that.

Share information about your business with new customers so they get a feel for you. Remember, connecting with your customer is what creates relationships.

This new customer website page is the ideal place to include reviews highlighting unique features of your business or therapists. Start grooming client relationships with your customized website page.

Here's an easy way to format what your business offers.

Have a list of what new clients can expect or a Q & A section to address some of the common questions you get from potential new clients.

What to expect at (your business name here)?

Expect to work with an experienced massage therapist. Our therapists average 8 years in the field. Massage is a gamble; you never know what you'll get. You have a greater chance of having all your expectations met with a therapist who has more experience under their belt. Please arrive 10 minutes early for your first session in order to complete our client information form.

Expect your therapist to be attentive to your needs and to be quiet during your session. This is your time to relax and loosen tight and stressed muscles. We do not engage in talking.

Expect no upselling during or after your session.

Expect no sales pitch or membership selling.

At the end of your massage, you will receive a bottle of water and our profound gratitude for your business.

What people are saying about (your business name here)?

My massage therapist was so fantastic! I was gifted a massage gift card from my husband. I made an appointment when I had a really stressful week at work.

I had quite a few knots in my back muscles, but felt completely relaxed when all was done! I got the stone massage which was incredible. I will be back again. - Bethany

If you have online scheduling, create a tab or category for new customers.

Okay, so you're probably wondering, if someone books a 60-minute massage under the regular pricing, do you bring up your new customer discount?

Do you have to offer new customer specials to everyone new?

It's your call. Many businesses won't suggest discounts if the customer hasn't asked about them. They will charge the price of the service the customer booked.

One way to determine whether a customer is researching first timer offers is to have your new customer promotions a little different.

Have the name of the package unique or the length of service different.

Creating two new customer offers can be smart advertising.

For example, perhaps you offer a new customer an 80- minute massage. If your regular prices don't include 80 minutes, you'll know the person calling wants the new customer discount.

Create a spa package.

For example: Celebration Package - Enjoy a 50-minute massage with warm, relaxing hot stones. New Customer offer only $65.00. (Regular price $85.00)

By changing the length of service or creating a spa package for new customers, you'll know the customer who booked wants a discount. If a customer isn't searching for new customer discounts, they will book a basic 60 or 90-minute massage and pay regular prices.

Design Your Menu - Wellness Programs or Membership Programs

Let's examine another dimension of the massage therapy business; wellness programs.

Why offer wellness programs? What inspires customers to sign up for such programs?

A price conscious consumer will examine your prices. If you offer a flat rate price for all your massages, there is no motivation to become a wellness customer.

Why do businesses want wellness customers anyway?

Wellness customers create loyalty. They are the definition of repeat business because wellness is a long-haul lifestyle choice. Developing relationships with clients can help businesses build and sustain long term success.

Repeat customers are beneficial for your business in many ways. They provide a dependable, consistent income stream. If your business has 50 customers on the wellness plan, that's 50 customers locked in each month.

One of the concerns with the massage industry or any service industry is low seasons or dry spells.

Research shows consumers spend more on massage therapy during certain months of the year. You have bills to pay regardless of the shifting sands of business fortunes. Repeat customers can give you much needed peace of mind with income you can count on.

Regular repeat customers also derive better health benefits under your hands. You become aware of their likes and dislikes, which enables you to tailor packages specifically for them. This leads to greater client satisfaction which will, in turn, strengthen your relationships.

A wellness program generates repeat business without hard sales pitches. The more value you create in your wellness plan, the more it motivates customers to get on board...or on the table.

You can offer different types of wellness plans. One way to go is a non-contract plan. This is an appealing option for a client nervous about being wedded to an agreement. Customers loathe manipulation and may have heard horror stories of customers who were sold into a 12-month deal with a massage business.

Clients often complain about some massage membership chain businesses. They feel as though they're perceived solely as a dollar sign and not a person. Here's the rub, a massage naturally releases feel-good hormones. After a massage, customers are riding the high of those happy hormones. Being pressed into a 12-month contract while under the influence of those feel-good hormones can leave the client with buyer's remorse.

Not all chain stores manipulate clients in this vulnerable state. The ones who do, however, create a negative impression of the industry among clients who come to feel like they've been played.

It's all down to communication. Customers can be turned off if a business is overly aggressive in trying to sell memberships. With a few wellness options in your arsenal, the customer can choose from your varied menu.

Some call this the soft sale. I call it "massaging the sale." Sorry, I couldn't help it!

You want to create a pressure-free environment, one that doesn't force an immediate decision.

It's a good idea to showcase the price benefits of wellness programs in your marketing materials. A framed flyer on your desk puts those benefits front and center where your customers can see them.

Here's another wonderful marketing tool to pollinate your customers' minds with wellness plans. Create business cards with your wellness plan printed on them. This is a terrific soft sale tool. Give each customer this business card. If it feels appropriate, take a few minutes to explain the options as you hand them the business card. This soft form of selling is sharing information without pressure to decide.

This is especially smart marketing if you have a therapist on staff who is a little timid. They can distribute the business cards without feeling pressured to close a membership sale.

If you would like me to send you a sample flyer, please email me at SabrinaTonneson@gmail.com. In the subject, request FREE flyer to promote wellness programs.

You can run promotions to get a big influx of wellness customers. For example, sign up for a six-month term and get a free 30-minute upgrade on the sixth month. Or, sign up for a six-month term and receive a free massage on the sixth month.

The more value you offer during the promotion, the greater the possibility of selling more memberships. If you want this promotion to be a one-time affair - use the words "Introductory Offer". This lets your customers know if they re-enroll in another six-month term, they won't be receiving the promotional offer again.

Design Your Menu - How to create a Membership Contract

There are no hard rules for contracts. You can customize them as you see fit.

Some businesses don't offer wellness plans because they're reluctant to wrangle with contracts and cancellations. The advent of the "bad online review" has made massage therapy businesses leery of contract arrangements. The last thing they want is a disgruntled customer burning the midnight oil on the internet to burn their business reputation.

It needn't be that way.

If a customer wants to cancel, you can decide how to handle it individually. If there's no interest in keeping them shackled to the contract, simply tell that customer you'll allow a one-time, penalty-free cancellation.

The reason a contract is beneficial, even if you don't plan to enforce it, is because it convinces your customers to come in monthly. You create a mutually beneficial exchange. They get the best prices, you get regular monthly customers.

If you have a wellness customer unable to keep their appointments, you can customize the arrangement. You can decide how you want to proceed case by case.

Worst-case scenario, you've processed two months of payments, but they never came in. Now, they are calling to say they want out and a refund.

Refunds are a headache for most businesses as they incur fees and extra paperwork.

One easy solution can be to tell your customer you will allow them to can cancel without penalties. Explain that you won't bill them for the balance of their contract. Let them know they will have an in-store credit of _ dollars.

If they're unable to come in, they can gift their store credit to a friend. The friend can use the store credit toward regular price services.

You always want to appear accommodating and non-confrontational. Instead of saying, "no, you signed a contract that says no refunds", outline what you can do for them. This is a customer service 101 tip.

Remember, if you have a customer asking for something and you are not sure how to respond immediately, tell them you need to discuss it with your partner. (Some people think if they operate the business alone they have no partner. A partner can be someone who is your sounding board. They can be a silent partner. They can be an emotional, supportive partner. You do not have to disclose who is your partner or partners.) You can tell them you will call them back in a day. Take some time and think about how you want to handle the situation.

If you would like me to send you a copy of a sample contract, please email me at SabrinaTonneson@gmail.com. In the subject, write sample contract.

Design Your Menu - Massage Therapy Enhancements

It's a common theme in this book; variety is the spice of life. Additional menu options can enhance your profits.

You can create more menu options with add-ons or a la carte options. Some businesses call them massage therapy enhancements.

To help explain this concept, think of a restaurant menu. Most menus offer the option of purchasing items a la carte. This gives the customer the option to customize the massage with enhancements of their choice. One great way to advertise your enhancements is to list them on a flyer prominently displayed in the room where customers fill out paperwork.

To spotlight your massage therapy enhancements, you can offer a regular price service with one FREE enhancement of their choice. When a customer comes in, you can hand them a laminated list of enhancements to review and select one. This will clue them in on the extra services your business offers.

Sample ideas you can use to create your own laminated flyer.

Massage Therapy Enhancements

Kansa Face Massage $15.00

Enjoy a slow relaxing face massage, which uses Kansa handheld contouring tool to balance the Ayurvedic doshas. Tightens and tones skin.

Face Mask $15.00

Deep cleaning clay face mask, followed by aromatherapy warm face towels. Includes moisturizing face massage. Great to clear sinuses, and opens energy channels in the face.

Deep Tissue Cupping on Back $15.00

Massage cupping works deeper by loosening adhesions, facilitating the muscles to operate more independent.

Cupping stimulates the skin by increasing circulation while separating fused tissue layer and draining lymph. Massage cupping can leave "hickey"-like marks on skin.

Hot Stone Foot Treatment $15.00

Warm relaxing hot towels foot wrap followed by hot stone foot massage. Soothes, hydrates and refreshes tired feet.

Hot Oil Scalp Massage $15.00

Hot moisturizing oils of jojoba, grapeseed, sesame, apricot and aloe vera used to massage scalp. Hot oil scalp massage feels fabulous and can help with dry skin or hair loss.

Muscle & Joint Therapy $15.00

Therapeutic massage for aching muscles and sore joints. Massage creme includes natural botanicals to help reduce inflammation, followed by cooling pain relief polar lotion. Polar lotion relaxes muscles with oils of wintergreen, peppermint and aloe.

Hot Stones $15.00

Warm relaxing hot stones help to release tension from tight and sore muscles. Heated hot stones help you to go into a deep state of relaxation.

Pick one targeted muscle group 1) neck/back 2) legs/feet or 3) arms/hands

What are some additional massage therapy enhancements options?

Massage Face Cupping

Asian Spoon Face Massage

Gua Sha Massage

Kansa Wand Contouring Sugar Scrub

Peppermint Masque Foot Treatment

Hands & Feet Shea Butter Moisturizing Treatment

Cold Stone Therapy

Salt Stones

Urgent Scheduling - extend your hours to accommodate client (some therapists will accommodate clients and come in after hours and charge after-hour rates)

To get more ideas - browse spa menu websites on the Internet.

Design Your Menu - Birthday Offers

One great marketing tool is to offer birthday specials. If you know your customer's birthdate, you can email them birthday greetings and make them a birthday massage offer.

If you don't collect birthdate information, no worries. You can create a page on your website especially for birthday massage offers.

However, be on the lookout for the fake birthdays, clients trying to scam a promotional offer. To get around that, politely ask the client to show photo ID at the time of the appointment to verify the birth date.

There are many ways to create birthday offers. For your regular monthly customers, you might want to gift them with something even more extravagant, for example, a free 30-minute upgrade. This way you'll still earn some money on the appointment.

Some businesses will gift a whole session to their regulars. It depends on your business. Usually the customers who are gifted with either a free 30-minute upgrade or free 60-minute massage tip very high at that appointment. It helps breed loyalty when customers feel valued.

Another basic way to give regular or new customers a birthday gift is to offer a great package for them, perhaps a 75-minute massage with aromatherapy scalp massage, peppermint hot towel wrap and warm relaxing hot stones. Regular price $129.00 - Birthday special $69.00!

You can stipulate a specific time within which the birthday customer must use this offer. This could be 15 days before or after their birth date. That gives the customer a 30-day window to get their appointment scheduled.

Couples massage is another great idea for birthdays as someone is usually treating the birthday person. The birthday couples massage allows them to enjoy the gift together. It's a fun activity to share and they get to shed some stress in the bargain.

Design Your Menu - Referrals

Do you offer referrals? What are the benefits? How can you use referrals to build your business quickly?

First of all, referrals are one of the best marketing tools bar none! The reason referrals are marketing gold is because the new customer already feels they will be satisfied. Remember, massage is a gamble. When you go to a new business, you can't predict the experience. You can't be sure if you'll like the location, the atmosphere, the staff or the style of massage.

If someone has recommended a therapist or a business, that recommendation removes risk as it is an endorsement by someone who has already sampled the goods. So how can you reward customers who do the advertising for you?

First, recognize that advertising costs money. It's better to invest your money on guaranteed customers rather than maybe customers. There's no reward for a referral unless a customer comes in, whereas with advertising, you pay for ads regardless of how much business comes your way.

The other benefit of referrals is you show your customers you value and appreciate their word of mouth recommendations.

One great way to get your customers to invest time and energy promoting your business is to offer a new customer special, and then give the client making the referrals a reward.

Some will offer a $10.00 in-store credit for each referral.

One business owner I mentored decided to offer a whole session, a 60-minute massage for each referral. Her regular prices are higher than average price. For example, she charges $95.00 for 60 minutes instead of the $75.00 going rate in her area. Even though her prices were higher than average, she created extra value for her customers.

She takes her time with each customer and often gives him or her an extra 5 to 10 minutes. She does a wonderful intake/communication before each session starts, therefore, she is able to customize and deliver what the client is looking for. She includes the extras in her treatment, without any up charges. She has raving customers who are more than excited to tell their friends and family. Her business grew quickly with her one free massage for each referral program. She consistently does 10 appointments per week (her goal), and she's booked out several weeks in advance. She has the 'reward creates reward' down to a science!

One idea to accelerate business growth is to offer a temporary referral promotion. Let's say your normal reward for referrals is one free therapy enhancement. You can offer: for the month of (whatever the month is) all referrals receive 1 Free Therapy Enhancement and $20.00 in-store credit. If a customer refers 3 friends who come in that month - they will have an instore credit of $60.00 and 3 Free Therapy Enhancements to use.

This can encourage customers to talk to their friends, family and co-workers. It creates momentum!

The bigger the promotions or offer you make, the greater the incentive for your clients to get out there and sing your praises. You can have a contest. Offer a discount for each referral, and a free massage for the client who brings in the most referrals during the specified time.

This, again, can encourage customers to go and sell your business. Some people enjoy the challenge of winning and will be motivated to go get you those referral customers.

Design Your Menu - Loyalty Reward Program

Loyalty is a highly valued commodity in the massage therapy business. It's a trait you'll definitely want to honor in your customers. There are several ways you can do that.

If you create loyalty reward business cards, they might put the card in their wallets. They will see the card randomly and recall how much they enjoy your massages. The business card is a visual reminder.

Loyalty rewards show your customers you acknowledge their importance to your business. It's also a great selling tool. Some people may forget you offer a loyalty program, particularly if it isn't printed on your menu or highlighted on your website.

If a client received their 3rd massage, you tell them with their next massage that they get their reward (provided you offer rewards on every 4th massage).

This motivates people to schedule sooner rather than later as everyone loves a reward!

Here are some sample ideas of loyalty rewards.

Buy 3 massages get free 15-minute upgrade on 4th.

Buy 3 massages get a free enhancement on 4th massage.

Buy 3 massages get 4th massage half off.

Buy 5 massages get 6th one free.

Buy 5 massages and receive 30-minute free upgrade on your 6th massage.

(They would pay for 60 minutes but they would receive 90 minutes)

Financial Goals

As you work on your marketing game, you always want to keep your financial targets in your sights. What are your basic needs, expenses and financial goals?

Business owners work backwards. That means you come up with your end total first, and then figure out how to create the sum.

For example, if your basic income need is $500.00 a week, $500.00 is going to be the sum. Next you create formulas and strategies to get to that figure.

Most businesses have 2 or 3 sum goals. The first sum total covers the bare minimum, that's just the scratch to pay your overhead.

The next dollar goal will be higher, your average sum. It includes the bare basics and some extra dollars to give you a bit of wiggle room. Wiggle room includes money for unexpected expenses as well as rainy-day savings for slow periods.

Your 3rd sum total will be your financial success goal. This total will reflect revenues to think big with business upgrades, a bonus for yourself, or that miniature donkey you've had your eye on for some time; whatever your mind can conjure. (smile)

These sum totals and goals will change over time.

Smart businesses re-evaluate their sum totals and goals every 90 days.

How much do you need to earn a week to meet your sum goals?

Bare basic sum goal? _____

Average sum goal? _____

Financial success goal? _____

Evaluating the Current State of Your Business

Continually take the pulse of your massage therapy operation.

How is your business currently operating?

If you already have clients, let's examine what percentage of your business is already filled.

How many appointments a week can your business offer?

How many appointments a week is your business averaging?

If your business can do 50 appointments a week, and you're averaging 10 appointments a week, you have an 80% opportunity for growth.

What percentage of growth is available for your business?

Now we want to cross-reference our sum totals with your existing income.

How much income are you currently averaging per week?

If your 10 appointments are averaging $700.00 a week and your basic sum is $500.00/week, your business is in a great place for growth without stress.

A calculation of the numbers will help determine the health and prospects for your business. It's important to know the current state of your business.

An assessment will help you determine how much vigor you apply to marketing and promotions. If your business is in crisis mode, there will be more of an incentive to offer bigger promotions. You will also want to invest more time in marketing. If you are currently investing 2 hours a week marketing - passing out flyers, posting on social media, etc. You might want to invest 3 or 4-hours marketing. Temporally invest more time in marketing.

One problem that some businesses experience is they've not planned their marketing and financial strategy. The business is not earning enough to pay the overhead and panic ensues.

The typical panic response is price cuts for all services. It's possible to oversaturate customers with regular discounted specials. This can hurt the business because now the customers expect to only pay the discounted prices.

Understanding the power of pricing is crucial. Learning how to strategically offer discounts and designing thoughtful menus is important to the health of your business.

If your business is currently struggling, it's not too late. You can restructure your operation and attract new customers as well as create different relationships with existing customers who only pay discounted prices.

For example, you can turn your price conscious customer into a wellness plan customer.

Research and Raising Prices

Next, let's gather some information. If you haven't already researched other businesses, now is the time.

Google 'massage' and scrutinize massage businesses in your area. Call each business or scout their websites. Research chiropractors, fitness centers and day spas as well. Make notes of each business and their prices. You also want to study their menus. Do they offer a variety of services? Do they have a specialty service? Do they have a signature massage package? Do they have wellness or membership programs? You want to ingest and analyze all of this information.

One business owner felt uncomfortable raising her prices until she did this homework. She was shocked to discover other businesses charged over $20.00 more for the same services. She realized if she raised her prices, she could save for a much-needed vacation. She also got excited about upgrades she could buy for her business.

Prices can have a psychological effect on owners. Many make the mistake of assuming the price of the service is what they earn per hour. They forget to factor in all the hours that go into operating the business. Hours invested in marketing, researching, accounting, cleaning, managing, social media connections, customer service, appointment setting, etc.

If you track all the hours you invest in your business each week, including the time you deliver the hands-on massage, you'll work out what you really earn per hour.

Most business owners often get an unpleasant surprise when they take the time to calculate their real hourly wage.

One business owner I consulted with was apprehensive about raising her prices. We develop a strategy to allow her regular customers to be grandfathered in for 6 months at existing prices, while new customers paid the new prices. She had never considered the idea she could raise prices for new customers and allow specific clients to keep current prices.

Yes. Business owners can customize their pricing. Create strategies that make it easy for you to raise your prices.

Sample Menu Plan

I've got some homework for you.

What is the average price in your area? _____

What is your lowest price you're willing to accept for a customer who signs a contract or buys a package of 6 or more? _____

Are you willing to add services to your menu? _____

Will you be using therapy enhancements to create packages or offer add-ons? _____

Are you going to offer a promotional reward (temporary or permanent) for referrals? _____

How fast do you want to grow your business? _____

The faster you want to grow your business, the more promotions you'll want to offer. This is a great time to make temporary offers.

Example: one-month big rewards for referrals. ($25.00 store credit for each referral)

One-month promotion, offer great prices on package of 3 (to be used in 3 months or some expiration that is sooner rather than later - perhaps allow the package to be shared with friends/family).

Do you plan to have more appointment slots available in the near future? (Perhaps hiring more staff or adding more hours yourself)

This is a sample homework.

20 slots available a week - currently filling 10 slots each week. Average price in my area $65.00/hour

Therapist is currently charging $60.00/hour.

The lowest price therapist is willing to work is $55.00/hour

Yes, to adding a variety of items on menu.

Yes, to temporary offers to grow business faster.

This is a sample pricing and menu for the above sample homework results.

Raise price from $60.00 per hour to $69.00 per hour.

Contact regular customers and let them know you are raising your prices. You can grandfather them in at same prices for 3 months or longer. Customers can be offered the option to be on a monthly wellness plan without prepaying or signing a contract. You can customize any arrangement that works for you. Make sure you are clear on the details.

One business owner I mentored had a few monthly clients. She told them she would grandfather them in with the original price. She never told them they would need to keep coming in monthly to keep the agreement active, nor did she give them a timeline for the agreement.

Fast forward, some of those customers stopped coming in regularly. When they do come in, they wanted the original price. This business owner is now very busy with higher paying customers, but she honors the price with those customers. She learned an important lesson: get clear on the details, before you make an offer to someone.

Sample Menu

Regular Price

$69.00 per hour

New Customer Special

60-minute massage plus one massage therapy enhancement of their choice.

Only $59.00

Regular price for this service is $69.00 for massage and $15.00 for the complimentary enhancement upgrade = $84.00 (New customers save $25.00)

Wellness Programs

Option 1 - Return within 30 days and automatically get $5.00 off. No contract.

Option 2 - 3-month term $60.00 each (prepay $180.00 or charge their credit card on the 1st of each month)

Option 3 - 12-month term $55.00 each - (prepay or charge their credit card monthly)

Spa Packages: Pick names and content for each spa package.

Relaxation Package

60-minute massage with deep relaxing hot stones, aromatherapy scalp massage and hot towels - regular price $99.00

On Sale $75.00

Tranquility Package

75-minute customized massage, including warm relaxing hot stones, hot oil scalp massage and deep moisturizing peppermint, shea butter hand and foot massage - regular price $149.00

On Sale $99.00

Ten Dollar Tuesdays

All services are $10.00 off on Tuesdays.

(Not Valid for Wellness Customers)

Referral Program

$10.00 in store credit for each person a client refers.

This menu and new prices actually allow the business owner to earn more money. She's only offering her lowest prices to the customers who will come in monthly with a twelve-month agreement. She no longer offers a flat rate $60.00 massage.

This new price structure generates more business and more profits as she is able to target to a larger audience.

She'll take a temporary loss on the in-store referral credit, but she will be getting new customers without coming out of pocket to advertise. She will also be deducting the in-store credit from her new higher price of $69.00 instead of $60.00. She will be creating relationships and loyalty with her new and existing clients.

Tuesdays is her slow days and she averaged 1 appointment. She will take a slight loss on Tuesdays, but she is happy to have her one slow day booked. As her schedule becomes busier, she may change her Tuesday offer.

Pricing and Menu Worksheet

Research at least 5 other businesses' prices and menus.

Business

Name

60 min price

90 min price

Membership Program?

New Customer Offer?

Spa Packages?

Menu Options: Write your prices and create options. Delete or cross out what you don't want to include.

Add your own ideas. Once you get an overall sense of what services you want to offer and what prices you want to charge, create your own customized menu.

Massage Prices (pick how many options you want to offer).

30 minutes

45 minutes

50 minutes

60 minutes

75 minutes

80 minutes

90 minutes

Specialty Services (can include sports massage, couples massage, reiki energy, work, lymphatic treatments, pregnancy etc.).

New Customer Offer

(Pick if you want 1 or 2 new customer offers. Good idea is to have a shorter service for lower price and longer service for higher price. This will allow two different types of customers to book.)

Option 1

Option 2

Wellness Plans (membership)

Option 1 - return in 30 days no contract

50 or 60-minute price?

80 or 90-minute price?

Option 2 - six-month term (paid at beginning of each month or prepaid package - create what you want to offer)

50 or 60-minute price?

80 or 90-minute price?

Customize your own wellness offer

Spa Packages (create different lengths of time with different enhancements upgrades included)

Option 1

Option 2

Option 3

Massage Therapy Enhancements – Add-ons

Referral Program

Loyalty Program

Success Stories

When Sabrina suggested I add a menu to my business, I didn't think it would be useful. I rent a room in a professional building and I work for myself. I decided to try it and, to my surprise, I noticed a difference right away.

My new customer offer was a hit and I received a big influx of new customers. My birthday offer is another big hit. I found more and more of my clients recommending me to their friends.

I make more money now.

My most popular service is the 60-minute Lavender Infusion package where my customers get hot stones and aromatherapy. Customers love this package and I make more money for this session!

Plus, I have almost 20 people who are on my wellness plan. I am staying busy, even during slow times.

I really underestimated how much value I would receive by offering a menu. I am so happy I tried it! Menus are one of the best-kept secrets in the therapeutic massage industry. - Carol Jons LMT

I work for myself out of my home. When Sabrina encouraged me to bring in a menu for my services, I felt silly. Menus are for bigger businesses and day spas.

I was skeptical, so I decided to start with only 3 items on the menu.

1. New Customer offer 2. Ultimate Relaxation offer (90-minute massage with all the extras) and 3. Package of 3 (prepaid package).

I typed up my menu and I started to hand it out to customers, as well as I started to leave my menu around town. The first few weeks I didn't notice a change, but then I started getting calls about the new customer offer. Some of my regulars decided to upgrade and try the Ultimate Relaxation package. I would say over 50% of them continue to book that package now.

I am seeing results with this menu. I am going to expand my menu again and give my existing customers and potential new customers more options. I really like this marketing plan. - Jan Blanshan - LMT

We already had a list of services when I hired Sabrina for consulting. Working with Sabrina, we realized we were not making the extra money for upgrades because our staff was already including upgrades for free in the basic massage service.

We needed to restructure to get everyone on same page. I hired Sabrina to lead a meeting with my staff. She was able to professionally articulate the importance of everyone being on same page. She motivated the therapists to want to sell upgrades and gave demonstrations on how to get upgrades without sounding pushy.

One example is to offer a customer a one-time sample of an upgrade. We gave the therapists bonuses for selling upgrades. This extra income encouraged the therapists to sell the upgrades.

After the staff meeting, I noticed a difference. First, our staff is now aware it is not okay to offer the extras if the customer is not paying.

We are seeing more and more upgrades. Sabrina suggested we offer a game for upgrade sales. Not a competition game between the therapists, but a game where everyone can be a winner. If therapist sold 5 or more upgrades a week - they got a bonus $10.00 gift card to Starbucks. The therapists all love their coffee! If they sold 9 or more upgrades a week, they got a $20.00 gift card. We played this game for 3 consecutive weeks and we noticed each week therapists were selling more and more. Everyone was a winner.

It was a genius idea as it really helped the therapists get comfortable talking about upgrades. Now, our regular customers are requesting upgrades on their own as they love them!

I highly recommend calling in support. It is wonderful to have an outside person come in with new eyes and offer insights as well as motivation. Thanks

Sabrina! You clearly love massage and business; your passion is contagious! - Vicky Dale - LMT

Sabrina is available for consultations. Consultations are a wonderful tool for any individual business or company.

Hire Sabrina today and get help with any of the following.

Increase profits

Feeling stuck

Staff problems or challenges

Take your business to next level

Get more customers

Need motivation

Customizing your menu and prices

Create new marketing strategies

Hiring

Customer service

Staff training

Growing pains

Team energy and harmonizing

For more information and a special offer, please go to www.MassageMarketing101.com

Massage Marketing

Don't Leave Money On The Table

Book 2

Sabrina Tonneson

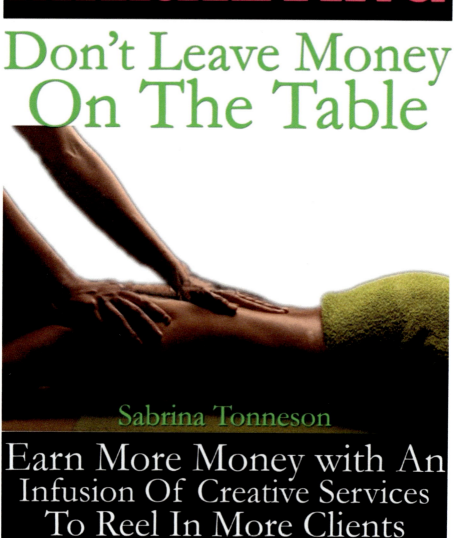

MASSAGE MARKETING

Don't Leave Money On The Table

Sabrina Tonneson

Earn More Money with An Infusion Of Creative Services To Reel In More Clients

Introduction

You've just delivered one of your signature, stress-obliterating massages. The client gushes about your magic fingers as they leave the table. There goes another satisfied customer.

Yet, as you clean up the massage room, you're left with a niggling feeling something isn't quite right. Your massage therapy practice isn't garnering the same satisfaction your clients walk away with.

Stuck in a financial rut, the profits your hands work so hard to earn aren't materializing.

Well, the good news is all of that is going to change! With the application of the remedies detailed in this book, you'll start to see a turnaround in your business fortunes with some solid, money-spinning strategies!

You've got the talent and work ethic, no doubt. A critical component for a wildly successful massage therapy practice, though, is taking the leap beyond the basic flat rate massage.

Sticking with a basic flat rate massage is the surest path to flat lining business growth. Creating a services menu can be one of your most effective massage marketing tools. You need to grasp the power of options and the importance of reaching out to a variety of customers with irresistible packages. The key to attracting better profits is tailor-made offerings for different client demographics.

Many massage therapists funnel all their energies into their craft, but need help conceptualizing ideas to create a menu. The profit boosting principles explored in this book allow anyone in the massage therapy business to transform the performance of their practice.

This book, Massage Marketing: Don't Leave Money on the

Table is the follow up to Massage Marketing: Boost Profits, Earn More, Work Less By Implementing a Strategic Pricing Menu.

It demonstrates why a menu and creative packaging are key stepping stones to financial success. While some folks are on board with the idea of creating a business menu, imagining what services they can offer is where they get stuck. Well, have no fear! I'm here to teach you how to create and showcase packages in an appealing way.

My name is Sabrina Tonneson and I have over two decades of massage therapy experience. From head to toe, I'll give you ideas to make every inch of skin your fingers travel count. You'll learn how to conceive wonderfully decadent packages to lure clients on both tight and open budgets. It's time to turn your business into a real money-making proposition!

Grow Your Business Quickly

That's what we all want, a business that shows robust growth with healthy profits. One of the best ways to germinate that growth is with the development of a spa package to accommodate a variety of services. Don't limit your scope for expansion by obsessing about your budget or room size.

Tech titan and Apple co-founder Steve Jobs' vision was born in a garage, so you shouldn't allow your current circumstances to dictate your future successes. The most important thing is getting to work on your vision with packages that fit a range of budgets. That is a sure-fire path to kick starting your healthy income breakthrough.

Temporary offers are a smart marketer's secret. Test out an idea with a temporary offer. The test is not only for feedback from clients but also from the massage therapists. One business I consulted wanted to introduce the popular sugar scrubs. The business invested in the sugar scrub product and started to promote. Customers enjoyed it, but the therapists did not! All the therapists complained the sugar scrub was challenging to remove. Even after they washed their hands, the sugar crystals somehow seemed everywhere. If a product is hard to remove or clean, it can create challenges for the rest of the treatment. The business tried a foot masque instead of sugar scrub and the therapists were happy. Customers liked both. If your team of therapists are unhappy with a product, it is not a win win. Luckily the business did not print materials with sugar scrub and they were easily able to modify the offer to design a win win package.

Another benefit of a temporary offer is to determine how much product you use. If a treatment is taking more product than you expected, the profits might not be large enough for the package to be an asset. If the price of package is too high, and customers are not buying the package, the products can get old and expire.

Temporary offers allow you to tweak your package. You can experience through trial and error not only what you want to include in the package, but how much you want to charge for the package.

#1 Tip for Success

Become a customer. Imagine yourself as a massage therapy customer. Stay with me here. One of the best things you can do to get repeat clients is to become a regular massage customer yourself!

If you don't have a lot of folding money lying around for monthly massages, you can trade them. Trading massages, though, isn't the same as being a regular paying customer. When the money leaves your pocket after an hour of service, your expectations of what constitutes a good massage experience change.

My sage advice to all massage therapists is get a massage every month by someone new. When you sample new businesses and new therapists, you become connected to the service and what your customers feel. It's a toss of the dice, you can't be sure if you'll love or hate the experience. Trying out different therapists expands your exposure to a variety of techniques. Some techniques will sizzle while others fizzle. You need to go out there and find out which is which.

One therapist whom I had coached admitted, after a lengthy interrogation under hot lights, that she did not get regular massages. (Smile)

After some prodding, she resolved to get one or two massages per month. Well, this therapist returned to me with glowing reports that her business increased. As the therapist become the massaged, she felt a shift. She confessed she had been feeling like a hypocrite advising her clients to make regular visits, while she herself often waited several months between massages.

Once she started getting regular massages, though, and began to absorb all of the benefits, this gave her practice an added authenticity.

Another welcome result of her massage excursions was a noticeable increase in tips! It suddenly dawned on her that when she took the time to keep her own mind and body in balance, she had more to offer to her clients. This, in turn, enabled her to extract greater enjoyment from her practice. Thus, began a happy deluge of compliments, tips and that golden ticket; referrals!

Now, this next story will sound strange, but bear with me. One experience that really shaped my business and helped me quickly multiply repeat clients was receiving an awful massage. That's not to say you should go in search of a massage therapist who will knead your back like dough, but here goes: I rolled out of bed one morning with a sore, tight neck. I needed massage therapy! There was a place charging more than I was wanted to part with, but it was the only business with an opening.

During my consultation with the therapist, I advised that she dedicate the entire session to my neck and back. Peculiarly, she had other ideas and kept trying to pressure me into a full body massage. I sensed she was a bit of a novice and didn't know how to give a neck and back massage only. I finally let her talk me into doing my arms because she was mule-stubborn about what she wanted to do.

The massage was average, but the whole time she was doing my arms I was annoyed. I didn't want my arms done. My fingers weren't a priority at that moment. My neck was in pain, and now my massage therapist was another pain in my neck. It doesn't take an expert to know that if your massage therapist leaves you feeling irritable, that's the exact opposite of what you'd expect from a session.

That dreadful experience really helped me appreciate the customer's point of view. Give your clients what they ask for.

But wait, there's more! During yet another memorably disappointing session, I had requested extra work on my hamstrings and quadriceps. A punishing stair machine workout left my legs quite sore. The therapist was skilled enough and gave a great massage.

There was one exception, though, she spent one or two minutes on each leg. If someone asks for extra work on two muscle groups and you have 90 minutes, how much time would you spend on those muscle groups? Yes, it does sound like a math quiz question, but I was so irritated. One of two things happened, she either ignored my request or didn't care. Either way, I lost out! Just recounting those incidents gives me hankering for a massage...from a therapist who listens!

Those unpleasant experiences really helped me grow my customer base quickly. They taught me that knowing what not to do is as important as knowing what you should do. There is no doubt that in massage school my massage tormentors were taught to be attentive to their customers. People often fail to learn these important lessons until they experience the frustration first hand. When it comes to squandering someone's time and money, it gets personal.

To this very day, I try to get a weekly massage, auditioning a new business every month. Chiropractors, fitness centers, day spas and massage centers; I try them all with an open mind. This wealth of experience allowed me to rapidly grow my business. I can't put too fine a point on this: being a consumer of the service you sell is the best advice I have for any massage therapist.

Create the Ambiance - Lighting

Building up massage experiences to influence the quality of your own massage therapy practice is key. Just as important, though, is the environment you create for your clients.

Remember, a massage is supposed to be a relaxing experience, a manipulation of the muscles to chisel away tension in the body and mind. If the lighting in your massage therapy room can compete with a stadium on Super Bowl night, here's a hint: take it down a notch.

Bright lighting makes relaxation challenging. With a dimming switch, you can control the lamps and lighting in your massage therapy to create an environment conducive to relaxation and blissful repose. Dimmer switches are affordable and easy to use.

Create the Ambiance - Eye Pillow

Here is another exceptional value add-on to your practice: give eye pillows ago. A massage with an eye pillow is a low cost extra that can help your clients drift off into an ethereal state of dreaminess. Never heard of it? You don't know what you're missing. It's almost like being drugged, except you won't wake up in an abandoned warehouse surrounded by swinging meat hooks.

Amazon has a variety of eye pillows to choose from.

Here's a useful tip, heat your eye pillow. After you've finished the face and neck massage, place the warm eye pillow on your client's eyes. If you haven't tried this before, incorporate it into your next massage. Your customer will really go for them.

The darkness helps quiet frenetic minds and allows your clients to sink into a deep state of relaxation. Place a fresh Kleenex under the eye pillow for each client.

Create the Ambiance - Scents

Massage therapy is, in many ways, the seductive art of stimulating the senses. While you work primarily with the sense of touch, smell is another pathway to euphoric serenity. That's why you should use the gift of smell to create a warm, welcoming atmosphere.

There are many techniques to employ scents in your massage therapy practice. Spa diffusers are invaluable tools in optimizing your clients' sense of smell. Again, Amazon is a great marketplace to find diffusers of varying sizes and costs. You may want to buy a few diffusers depending on the size of your business and rooms.

At the beginning of the day, you can select the scent you want and drop essential oils into the diffuser water reservoir. You should use the same oils in all of your diffusers to create one uniform, pleasant odor throughout your business. Too much mixing and you might end up with a potpourri atmosphere. Some therapists go for a stronger bouquet, others like something understated.

Candles are another great way to perfume your business. You can light enough candles to create the right mood and scent, but not so many that it looks like a seance. It's important to observe all fire prevention protocols and make sure you have a functioning fire extinguisher if you intend to use scented candles.

The possibilities for experimenting with scents are really limitless. If you have a crockpot with hot towels, try placing a few drops of essential oils on your wet towels. When you open the lid to get a hot towel, the pleasing odors will billow out.

I like to swing the hot scented towel near to the client's head. The smell of peppermint permeates the room and the client's senses. It can even clear blocked sinuses.

Aromatherapy and massages have been at the heart of some truly amazing experiences. In fact, my memory has preserved one such experience in California. The massage in question was approaching the end. I was lying face down when, suddenly, the unmistakable scent of peppermint found my nose. It wasn't there during the massage, but it suddenly materialized, announcing itself like the first day of spring!

It was refreshing and welcoming. When the treatment ended and I was getting dressed, I went into detective mode. I snooped around to see if I could spot the diffuser from whence this intoxicating aroma had issued. There was nothing to be found. Never one to be shy, I asked the therapist how she got her scents game so strong. She revealed her mystery technique; using just a few drops of essential oils in her palms, she deftly waved them beneath the face cradle. In waving her hands, the peppermint aroma pervaded the atmosphere. It was mind-blowing how such a simple technique could create a valuable add-on to a massage therapy practice.

Imitation is the sincerest form of flattery and I adopted that modest, yet powerful technique of building an aroma-filled environment for my clients. My efforts didn't go unnoticed, commendations from customers flowed in abundance. This technique is particularly useful because some clients' sinuses become congested when they lie face down. The peppermint trick relieves the blockage, and the clients absolutely love it.

Obviously, I am a huge fan of scents. Not everyone is the same. You may have a customer who dislikes scents or is allergic. As always, accommodate what is in the best interest of your client.

Create the Ambiance - Layout and Design

There is one final point of discussion when it comes to making your business warm and welcoming. You may be familiar with the phrase, "You never get a second chance to make a first impression."

Ask yourself, what's the first impression you want your customers to have when they walk into your practice? If increased profit and repeat business is your sort of thing, you want to be sure that your clients are exposed to the most appealing design and layout you can muster.

Neat and tidy is the first place to start. If your practice appears cluttered and you look disheveled, a client is liable to extrapolate that first impression to the quality of service you offer. If you're finding items in your office which cannot justify their presence there, they should be discarded. When clients walk into your practice, they should immediately feel as though they have stepped off the streets and onto a cloud.

As you may not be the best judge of your business's character, invite some friends over and have them give you their unvarnished impressions of your space.

If you're thinking about a business an upgrade, a simple yet tasteful paint job could do the trick. You don't need to break the bank to create the most welcoming atmosphere.

Create the Ambiance - Massage Table

Here's an important question, how comfortable is your massage table? Think about it, your clients will be laid out on this table for between 60 and 90 minutes. A comfortable table can be a soothing centerpiece asset to your practice.

Invest a little thought and time into making your massage table a plush cradle of comfort, and watch as your clients literally deflate...ahhh...as they slip into a state of relaxation bordering on catatonic.

If you've ever been on a hard massage table, then you'd know it's pure torture. Indeed, one of my worst massage table experiences was on a cruise ship. The price was double precisely because it was a cruise ship so I was expecting decadent pampering on a massage table that should have made me feel I was being levitated by sorcery.

Instead, I was laid out on a narrow plank of a table that was as hard as a diamond. I've tried massages on three different cruise ships and the tables were all invariably awful. I might as well have been laid out on the street. I love a good massage as much as anyone else, but to be crucified on a rock-hard table for 75 minutes is too great a test of my faith.

So how do you create a great massage table on a budget? Head off to a Walmart or Target-type store and, in the bedding section, pick up some foam for a single or double bed. If you buy for a double bed, cut or fold the foam.

Before putting on your sheets, lay out the foam. Next, you'll want to add some heat. For that, use a twin-size heating blanket.

Massage table heating blankets are usually twice the price, so if you use a twin-size you'll pay less. You can check out trusty old Amazon for some great deals. If you live in winter states, stores tend to offer their heating blankets on sale in the months of February and March. It's a good idea to pick up the sale item and keep an extra blanket in case one fails on you.

A twin-size mattress pad is also a good investment. The heat and the cushion from the foam will add that extra layer of dreamy comfort to your massage table.

If money's no object, then get the memory foam. It costs over $100.00, but good memory foam will give your clients a memorable experience. See what I did there?

I love to patronize massage businesses which use memory foam. When I get up on that table, I just drift off into a realm where all my troubles dissipate. Massage therapists usually have a hard time getting me off such a table!

Create the Ambiance - Neck Pillow

You should offer a pillow to elevate your customer's' head after a neck, scalp and face massage. Lying flat on your back isn't the most comfortable sensation. Throw a pillow in there and the experience will be much more enjoyable for your clients.

You can use pillows as well as towels. Take a towel, roll it up, and place it beneath the neck. Some massage therapists purchase a hot towel caddy and store dry towels in them. They use a rolled up, heated, dry towel to place under the neck.

The Art of Hot Towels

You can buy a crockpot at one of those big box or general stores and use it for your hot towels and hot stones.

Here's how you do it: wet your hand towels and rinse them well. The more residual water in the towel, the hotter it will be. You can use hot towels in many ways; scalp treatments, face treatments, foot treatments and on the back.

One important thing to remember when working with hot towels is that they get cold quickly. Some massage therapists will wrap a foot in a hot towel, then go and massage the leg. By the time they return to the hot towel, it has cooled off. A cold wet towel on the skin is like having a large frog on your back. Don't ask me how I know that, just trust me, it is an unpleasant feeling.

In one unforgettable experience I had with a cold, soggy towel, my massage therapist started my session with a hot towel on my back. She was getting full points already. Ahh, it felt wonderful!

With the hot towel still on my back, she moved on to my legs. The towel cooled off and I started to feel cold. Ahhh, changed to ughh! I couldn't even enjoy the work she was doing on my legs as I could only think of this cold, wet towel/frog on my back. I finally had to ask, "could you please remove that cold towel from my back?"

Here's a neat trick to solving that problem. Put a heated towel on yourself and time how long it takes to cool down to the point of being uncomfortable. Then you will know firsthand how quickly the towel cools.

There are two great tips for using hot towels on the back.

Tip 1) Place a dry towel on the back first, then lay your hot wet towels on top of the dry towel. Do your compressions on the towels. When you go remove the towels, the client's back will neither be wet nor will it have a cold sensation from the air as the towel is lifted off.

Tip 2) Lay a wet towel on the client's back, do your compressions, then pull up your sheet. After you've raised the sheet, remove the wet towel. The sheet will prevent the cold air from chilling your client's back after the towel has been removed.

Don't do compressions on top of sheet with the hot towel underneath, as the sheet will absorb moisture from the towel. A damp sheet is no fun either.

Hot towels are the most affordable way to enhance a package. Towels can be washed and reused over and over again. You can be creative with towels. One customer had aching, sore forearms. I took a heated towel and wrapped it around her forearm and did compressions. She told me it was the best forearm massage she ever received.

Learning New Techniques

Massage therapists often create their signature massage. This is the massage by which customers come to know the therapist. There is a routine which becomes easy enough to perform on autopilot.

However, performing the same massage day in and day out can become quite tedious. One way to keep things fresh and to stay motivated is through the incorporation of new techniques.

One of the best open universities to learn new ideas is YouTube. Yes, YouTube is a fantastic resource, even beyond videos of precocious babies, mischievous cats and adorable baby cats.

You can research any massage technique under the sun, with thousands of free videos available with instructional tips. If you want to learn how to include hot stones in your massage practice, you can simply search hot stone instruction videos.

Instructional DVDs are also widely available if you want to narrow your search for useful training materials, you can visit Massage Warehouse or even Amazon and investigate new modalities. Workshops and CEU classes are also invaluable training resources.

I have discovered that therapists who set a goal of learning something new every month, feel more rejuvenated when they are working. They may or may not use a new technique they've picked up, but it gives them more options to pack into their box of tricks. Keeping an open mind and assimilating new techniques is a great way to keep the mind stimulated.

One therapist I coached decided to take a massage cupping course and was pleasantly surprised by how much she enjoyed it. Additionally, she was thrilled to see how this newly-acquired knowledge benefited her clients. This therapist offered clients a free sample of the service, and then developed it as an add on to her range of services.

Now over 20% of her clients regularly request this upgrade. She even reeled in a few new clients because she is one of the few businesses in her area offering massages cupping. Picking up additional skills enabled this therapist to increase her profits while maintaining healthy stimulation of her mind.

Get Raving Fans with Hot Stones

Hot stones are a popular item in the massage business. The return on your investment will be over 1,000-fold. Customers absolutely love them. The stones are versatile as you can use full hot body stones or only concentrate the use of stones on certain muscle groups or focus areas.

A note of caution when working with hot stones, you will want to apply special care when working with the elderly. As we age, our skin becomes thinner and less resilient. If you are working with an elderly client, it's a good idea to go easy on the heat. You want to relax, not cook your client. I would recommend having your clients sign a release form in which they agree to communicate if the stones are too hot or are in any way a discomfort.

Hot stones are very flexible in their applications. Try out a massage using hot stones yourself so you can get an appreciation for the many ways they can be used.

There are Marble cold stones, Himalayan salt stones and Corestones, all of which can be used for different treatments. You can build different packages around these stones, thereby, adding to your diverse list of services.

Cold stones are effective in reducing inflammation while Corestones are great for sports massages. One of my preferred treatments is combination stone face massage.

Using both marble cold stone and basalt hot stone feels divine. Customers leave raving reviews about the hot & cold stone face massage!

If you want to learn more about these hot stone options, you can Google them and watch them on YouTube, preferably before the baby, cat and baby cat videos.

Some people find their own stones in nature. Not all stones, though, are created equal. While some will be great for your massage therapy practice, others are better suited to construction or throwing through the windows of tiresome neighbors.

Before using your stones on customers, try them out on family and friends to double check whether they deliver the desired results. If after those experiments they still consider themselves your family and friends, you know you are good to go.

When it comes to heating the stones, the most effective tool I've ever used is a slow cooker. These can be bought at Walmart-type stores for a fraction of the cost of professional hot stone heaters. The benefit of a slow cooker is the temperature control range. You can find the temperature that works for you and control the settings.

Crockpots with only warm, low and high settings can be problematic in achieving a consistent temperature. The main downside to a slow cooker is size. If you are working with a tight space, it can be tough to find a small slow cooker that will suit your needs. If you are going to look into a professional hot stone heater on Amazon or massage products stores, you should know that many of them give off an unpleasant odor. Read the reviews carefully before settling on your chosen heater.

Beverages and Snacks

A nice touch for any massage therapy practice is the provision of complimentary beverages. In the winter, your customers will get a kick out of an offer of warm apple cider, hot tea or chocolate.

If you want to offer two or more packages for special promotions, like a half day packages for Mother's Day, give your customer a small break in between sessions with a complimentary beverage and snack. You can buy individualized size packages of nuts, candies or crackers. Fresh fruit is always a crowd pleaser.

Presentation, though, is of paramount importance. It just feels more self-indulgent when you can recline in a soft robe and enjoy a refreshing beverage or snack. It's that feeling of king or queen for a day that will keep your customers coming back for more. Serve their cold water or fruit juice in a nice glass. Cocktail glasses often look appealing, filled with a refreshing beverage.

You may also want to consider to-go cups for clients to take a beverage with them, especially in the winter months. Imagine receiving a wonderful massage then be given a complimentary cup of hot chocolate or warm tea on your way out the door. Fill of coffee maker with only hot water, then offer a selection of beverage choices. This extra will leave a lasting impression. These are the little things that make a big difference to your bottom line. Smart marketer's get repeat customers by going the extra mile on the little things.

Different Types of Packages

Packages for Face and Scalp:

Kansa Contouring Face Massage

Asian Spoon Face Massage

Hot Oil Scalp Massage

Hydrating Face Mask

Aromatherapy Face and Scalp Massage

Packages for Feet and Hands:

Hydrating Hand and Foot Shea Butter Treatments & Scents

Peppermint Foot Mask

Hot Stone Hand and Foot Massage

Sugar Scrubs

Foot Soaks

Paraffin Wax Hand and Foot Treatments

Full Body Packages:

Scented Hydrating Body Treatment

Vitamin Rich Body Treatment (with exfoliation)

Dry Brushing (dry brush gloves are easy to use and easy to clean)

Seasonal Body Treatments - seasonal scents

Stress Buster

Detoxifying Body Wrap

Bamboo Massage

Gentleman Massage Package

Sports Massage

Corestone Massage

Himalayan Salt Stones

Specialty Packages or Add Ons

Cupping

Raindrop Therapy

Cranial Sacral

Lymphatic

Energy Work

Matrix Energetics - Two Point

Access Conscious - Run Bars

Reiki

Western & Eastern Massage Mixture

Trigger Point

Shiatsu

Thai

Pregnancy

Yoga Massage

Special Occasion Packages

Mother's Day - Father's Day

Sweethearts - Valentine's

Birthday Celebration

Anniversary

Any holiday - St Patrick's Day, Earth Day

Bridal Showers

Packages Names and Descriptions

Create a menu with different price points and length of services. Use catchy words to create interest and peak curiosity. Your package name and description are your sales team. Invest your time to create selling packages. If you do not like to write, hire someone to do the work for you. This is your chance to sell your services. I have included some samples for you.

Zen Package

Bliss out with a 50-minute scalp and face treatment. Package includes relaxing face massage with hot and cold stones. Moisturizing and hydrating pomegranate face lotion. Face massage and facial pressure points help release sinus and tension. Great for anyone with TMJ issues. Package includes hot oil scalp massage. Hot moisturizing oils of jojoba, grapeseed, sesame, apricot and aloe vera are used to massage the scalp. Treatment can help people with dry skin or hair loss. Hot oil scalp massage feels fabulous.

Kansa Facial & Foot Treatment

Facial treatment with Kansa wand. Tightens and tones skin, moves lymph and opens sinuses. Kansa face massage uses a handheld contoured tool to balance the Ayurvedic doshas.

Package includes foot massage with Kansa wand for whole-body balancing.

Bamboo Melt Away

Melt away pain and stress with a warm 75-minute bamboo massage. Package starts with dry brush massage to move lymph and exfoliate dead skin cells. Bamboo massage is a relaxing therapeutic massage that helps loosen the most stubborn knots and muscles. The warmth of the bamboo as well as long soothing techniques help diminish spasms and relieve stress. Pain and tension just fade away.

Celebration Package

Start your experience on a warm heated massage table. Release those tight and sore muscles with this 45-minute neck, shoulder and back massage. Package includes deep relaxing hot stones. Melt the tension away and celebrate your health and well-being.

Bamboo / Hot Stone Fusion Package

Experience the best of Eastern massage. Warm bamboo massage paired with hot stones. This combination massage package is a customer favorite! This therapeutic package releases sore and aching muscles while you feel drift into a place of peace and serenity.

Hawaiian Escape

Enjoy an escape to Hawaii. Start your Polynesian journey with a hydrating jasmine face massage. Your getaway includes a soothing Hawaiian Lomi Lomi massage with moisturizing tropical scents. One hour of uninterrupted me time to decompress and rejuvenate the body, mind and spirit.

Himalayan Salt Stone Massage

This healing massage uses heated Himalayan salt stones to reduce tension, relieve pain and inflammation. Through osmosis, the salt's minerals and nutrients naturally activate your healing mechanisms, allowing your body to restore itself to balance.

Chakra Balancing

Chakras are energy centers that affect our immune and endocrine systems. Negative information can adversely affect the body and spirit; this energy-balancing treatment uses gemstones to help clear the chakras, calm the mind and improve your body's ability to self-heal.

Lavender Infusion Package

60-minute session with calm, soothing lavender scalp massage.

Full body massage that includes hot stones on back. Hydrating lavender butter hand and foot treatment.

Bali Bliss Indulgence

Enjoy this ultimate 90-minute package of bliss. Select your favorite scent for your calming scalp massage. The package includes deep relaxing hot stones on back and feet. A mango sugar foot scrub sure to revitalize and balance your body.

Balanced Soles

Step into complete balance with a reflexology and acupressure foot package. Enjoy a peppermint foot masque followed by a hot towel foot treatment and hot stone foot massage.

Couples Massage Packages

Our couples signature massages include aromatherapy scalp massage. Pick your scent: *peppermint *lavender *orange *lemon *eucalyptus.

Hold hands as you de-stress together. Massage includes deep relaxing hot stones and hot towels. Massage releases feel good hormones and increases happiness. Couples who massage together, stay together!

Additional package names:

Relaxation Package

Tranquility Package

Serenity Package

Joy Package

Peace Package

Ultimate Package

(your business name) Signature Package

VIP Package

Royal Treatment Package

Mix and Match Package

Pick your favorites and customize the perfect massage for you! (have list of your therapy enhancements)

60 minutes - pick 2 therapy enhancements

90 minutes - pick 3 therapy enhancements

Express Massage

If you have limited time, enjoy one of our express massage for singles or couples. 30 or 45 minute massage focusing on one or two muscle groups of their choice.

Basic express couples massage is very popular. It is an affordable date idea. The express package allows people to try massage at lower price. Instead of advertising it as a budget massage, express massage is a nice way to offer a basic short session. The most common response is, they fall in love with massage and return for longer sessions with upgrades.

1) Half Day Package

Celebrate you with half day of pampering services. Pick any 2 of our treatments (have list of 50 or 60 minute packages). In between your treatments enjoy a light snack and beverage. 2 1/2 hours of Bliss!

2) Full Day Package

Indulge is a day of luxury.

You can allow customer to pick the treatments or you can have specific treatments. Include light lunch. You can allow them to pick from some menu options. For example, if you are going to bring in Subway, you can have them select their lunch choice at time of booking.

Don't Leave that Money on the Table!

As a massage therapist, you genuinely want to deliver the best for your clients. It is criminally negligent not to expect the same for yourself.

This book has given you many ideas that are guaranteed to help you transform your business fortunes. You can't be at your best for your clients if you aren't deriving satisfaction from your practice, both professional and financial.

The principles you've read in this book are the culmination of my many years of trial and error and struggle and success in the massage therapy industry. I am glad that you not only purchased this book, but took the time to read it through. This demonstrates a commitment on your part to take charge of your business future. All that is left is to take these ideas, get out there and put them into practice and watch your massage therapy practice flourish!

Jumpstart your business by hiring your own business consultant. Sabrina has a special offer for you found on her website.

http://www.massagemarketing101.com

Add On The Serenity

Book 3

Introduction

There is a huge opportunity to earn more money with upgrades. Upgrades are an amazing money-making tool. Clients love upgrades for several reasons. Upgrades allow your customers to try new treatments. Upgrades allows your clients to create and customize the perfect session for their likes and needs. Upgrades are fun for clients celebrating a special occasion.

Gift certificate customers love upgrades.

An average of 7 out of 10 gift card customers take advantage of upgrade options. Gift card clients often feel like they are receiving a free treatment, spending a little bit of their own money to experience an upgraded luxurious package is a common choice. Clients love having choices and options.

This book will show you how to create a list of upgrades. Learn how to make a list of different ideas and upgrade possibilities. A diverse list of upgrades allows you to appeal to a wide range of different types of clients and their different preferences. This book will show you how to sell upgrades with No pushy sales! Most therapists do not like hard sales. We are in the business of health and wellness, not hard sales. This book will teach you many easy ways to offer upgrades.

Every entrepreneur knows that the keys to sustainable prosperity and growth are a healthy curiosity and constant learning. Use this money-making tool to increase your daily profits! Don't leave money on your table by ignoring this popular opportunity.

Create Your Upgrade List

First of all, we want to get our creative juices flowing. Start making a list of ideas. Keep in mind, at this point we are only brainstorming. Start your creative thinking by making lists of ideas. Creativity creates momentum. As you turn on the flow of creativity the outpouring of ideas will go from a slow drizzle to a powerful stream.

One way to get your creativity flowing is to think of services you enjoy when you get bodywork. Ask your friends and family what they enjoy when they get bodywork. Google businesses around the world and see what other business are offering for upgrades and services. Go to massage and spa equipment stores or websites to see what products they sell.

Most people start the list with basic upgrade ideas.

Hot stones

Sugar scrub

Aromatherapy

Hot Towels

Cupping

Reflexology

These are great basic ideas. How can we dig deeper?

One way is to think of different parts of the body. Most people have their favorite areas. Create add ons that focus on specific areas.

Face & Scalp Upgrades

Some people love a scalp massage. They instantly melt away as their head is touched. Create a specialize treatment for clients who love their scalp touched.

For example, you could create an aromatherapy hot oil scalp treatment upgrade. In this upgrade, give your clients a choice of their favorite aromatherapy. Tell them their options and let them select.

One successful massage business displays 5 aromatherapy options on an attractive plate. They show the plate to their clients and ask them to pick their scent. Customers might smell each bottle and decide or customers might already know their favorite scent.

This interactive process engages the clients and gets them prepared and enthusiastic for their upgrade.

You can use an oil that is beneficial for hair, like grapeseed oil, coconut oil, etc. Drop the scents into the heated oil bottle. Slowly drop the hot oil on their 3rd eye. (You can buy plastic bottles for your oil at beauty supply stores. Heat your oil in an oil warmer or place bottle in your crockpot to heat.)

The oil will roll down into their scalp. Drop hot oil slowly all over their forehead. Their hair will become covered in oil. Massage in the oil. After the massage you can take hot towels and wrap the head with hot towels and do compressions on head.

You can wrap hair in dry towel when finished, or cover with a plastic hair net.

Add the aromatherapy of their choice on the hot towels before the session starts. When you open the crock pot to get the hot towels the smells will be amazing. The heat will feel fabulous, this scalp massage upgrade with send them into a state of bliss.

Hair masks and deep conditioning hair treatments are additional great upgrade options. Research different products. In the description include the benefits of the products used during the treatment.

Our creative juices are starting to flow. Keep going!

Some therapists include face massage with their bodywork and others do not. Having face upgrades guarantees your clients will be getting a face massage, which many clients like.

Hot stone face massage feels amazing and customers love their face massaged with hot stones.

You can leave warm stone on their 3rd eye at end of treatment and cover their eyes and forehead with a heated eye pillow.

Cold stone face massage is an excellent upgrades options for clients with migraines or inflammation. You can place small cold stone on top of eyes to help with puffiness. Leave them on their eyes while you are massaging different areas.

Combination hot and cold stone face massage upgrade is a customer favorite.

Other ideas for the face upgrades can include offering a face cleaning followed by a face massage using products that are excellent for face skin. Some of these products will cost more but might be worth it if they are effective skin care products and your customers love them. Plus, you charge more for the upgrades that cost you more money.

Research skin care products that are popular and beneficial. Take classes online or locally to learn more about skin care and face treatments.

Face masks are very popular. There are a variety of different types of face masks, like dead sea face mask, leave on hydrating face mask, vitamin C face mask, 24K gold face mask, clay face mask, etc.

There are also individual sheet face masks. These are nice as clients can select their favorite mask. If you buy the individual masks in bulk or discounted, you can sell the products.

Most massage therapists are not trained skin care experts. You will have certain rules and guidelines that your state will require. For example, if you offer a face treatment and your client asks for extractions, if you are not a licensed esthetician you cannot perform. Always check with you state to make sure any face treatment you offer complies with your state laws.

More face massage upgrades ideas include:

Kansa Wand Face Massage

Spoon Face Massage

Jade Roller Slimming Face Treatment

Belavi Facelift Massage

Face Cupping Massage

Thai Herbal Ball Face Massage

Body and Feet Upgrades

One difference between an upgrade and a spa package is the focus area to receive the upgrade. For example, a hot stone massage package would include hot stone massage over the full body, whereas a hot stone upgrade will include hot stones on a specific muscle group.

When offering body upgrades you can write the list of body upgrades choice, write the description then include this important piece:

Pick 1 targeted area - 1) back/neck 2) legs or 3) arms.

This is very important, as the customers who love these add ons often start to book specific packages to receive full body treatments. Think of these add ons as your sampler.

Pick 1 Targeted Area - 1) Back/neck 2) Legs Or 3) Arms

Body Upgrades Options:

Hot Stones

Cupping

Himalayan Salt Stones

Cold Stones

Icy Hot Therapy

Dry Brushing

Sugar Scrub

Body Polish

Bamboo Therapy

Thai Herbal Balls

Hand & Feet Upgrade Options:

Hand & Foot Hydrating Butter Treatment

Peppermint Foot Mask and Hot Stones

Hand Massage and Mask

Hand Soak & Foot Soak

Paraffin Wax Hand and Foot Treatments

Pick upgrades that accommodate your treatment room.

Do you have location for foot soaks? Do you have treatment room with sink? They have many products now for dry treatment rooms. If you want to do a body polish but you have a dry treatment room, google body polish for dry treatment rooms.

You can also contact massage and spa equipment stores and ask for product suggestions. There is a ton of information available online. The secret is to find products that are easy for you to use in your treatment room.

You want your clients to feel pampered as they indulge in their upgrades. If you are trying an upgrade that doesn't work for your treatment room, it will be awkward and take away from the experience.

When buying products consider a few things. How popular with that upgrade be? How quickly will you use the product? Will the product expire?

It is cost effective to buy larger containers, but if you do not use it all, it can be a waste of your dollars.

Sometimes it is better to buy a smaller size to make sure you like the product and you are able to sell the upgrades. If you do have a product that is about to expire, you can use that product strategically.

We will discuss how to do that in the chapter Selling Upgrades.

Some businesses love the upgrades and invest a lot of money in products.

One of the benefits of investing money in upgrades is your enthusiasm. When you add a service to your business, it can feel fun and exciting. It can help you look forward to going to work and giving the new treatments.

One thing to consider is the value of investing money in equipment or tools. Cold marble stones are not going to expire. There are many tools to buy that you can use over and over again. Think about what percentage of your investment you want to invest in products and what percentage you want to invest in tools or equipment.

Seasonal & Promotional Upgrades

One of the benefits of offering seasonal or promotional upgrades is the opportunity to experiment. You will have a chance to work with the product or tool and discover if you enjoy it. In the beginning, using new products or tools can feel awkward. It can take a few sessions to find your rhythm and develop a system or pattern that flows.

This is a great time to invite your family and friends to the table. Work out the new service kinks on the them. Smile! Massage humor never gets old.

Season and promotional upgrades are a great chance to discover what works and does not work for you. One business decided to offer sugar scrub upgrades. They invested money in large sugar scrub containers, they planned to promote and sell the service. The treatment rooms does not have a sink. The massage therapists found the product to be difficult. The little sugar sands seemed to stick to everything. Even after they washed their hands with hand towels, they couldn't remove all the little sands of sugar.

The therapists did not want to promote or encourage clients to try the upgrade as they didn't like doing it.

If you already purchased a large container of products, do not worry. There are ways you can still use it. Buying disposable gloves is one easy way to apply the product.

The point of that story is the benefit of seasonal products or promotional products.

Experiment and discover what is popular as well as discover if the therapists enjoy offering it.

Seasonal products are a fun way to engage clients and keep things new and fresh at your business.

One way to use seasonal products can be aromatherapy infused treatments. Each weather season is associated with different scents. Apple, pumpkin, spices, pine are all fall season scents.

You can buy or make products. Shea butter, coconut oil and aromatherapy make a wonderful hydrating shea butter hand and foot treatment. If you enjoy making products, you can discover great ideas on YouTube. There are many recipes and ideas available online. Google spa recipes for ideas and inspiration.

Another way to promote upgrades is to focus on holidays or local celebrations. Valentine's Month you can create rose or chocolate scented upgrades. You can get creative and offer fun upgrades. People like to indulge in limited time only services.

If you have a slow season or a slow month, you can use that time to create customer appreciation month. Create some new and different promotional upgrades for your clients.

You can use your upgrades to get business. During your customer appreciation week or month, you can offer each client a free upgrade as a thank you for being a regular customer. Create a special list of upgrades. If you have upgrades that are more expensive, like certain masks or skin products, do not include those upgrades on your free customer appreciation upgrade offer.

Use products or tools that do not cost you or cost very little. Clients love to feel like they are important to you and offering customer appreciation week is a great way to build loyal customers. Keep in mind you can offer customer appreciation week 2 or 3 times a year. Strategically plan your customer appreciation week during your slow times.

Outside the Box Upgrades

Add value and benefit to your client's session with outside the box upgrade ideas. Outside the box upgrades can include offers that will complement their session. They can be add ons your clients can use before or after the session.

If you have space at your wellness center offer a relaxation space upgrade. A popular upgrade is using the treatment room for a nap or meditation.

You can either create a meditation space or use the treatment room to allow your client time to decompress and sleep. These options are amazing before or after a session.

Some customers find it takes their body 20 to 30 minutes to relax. Clients like having the opportunity to listen to a guided relaxation meditation before their sessions begins.

Clients also fall asleep during their session. Some clients love knowing they can continue to sleep after the treatment. Offer a 30 minute or one-hour deep sleep upgrade.

If your treatment room is cozy and comfortable, you will find your clients do not want to leave. Soothing water sounds, aromatherapy scents, warm heated blankets, comfortable plush table all add to a decedent experience.

Create a space that allows your customer the chance to slip into a deep state of peace and relaxation.

Guided meditation selections. Outside the box upgrades can include a selection of guided meditations. Research meditation options. You will discover a diverse list of different type of meditations to appeal to a wide range of clients. You can have a meditation menu.

Hypnotism meditation are also popular. People can enjoy listening to a hypnotic meditation on body, health, money, relationships, parenting, etc.

The best time to hypnotize the mind is when the body is in a deep space of relaxation. Pair your bodywork with hypnotism meditations.

Subliminal messaging music upgrade. You can offer a subliminal message music to your clients. They can listen to this before, during or after the session, depending how you want to present the upgrade.

Snack and Beverage Upgrades

Another popular out the box upgrade is offering snack and beverages. This is especially popular with couples massages or friend spa day.

You can offer a selection of soothing hot teas, hot cider, hot chocolate, refreshing citrus drink, healthy fruit beverage, etc.

Some business offer wine, mimosas or cocktails. Check with your city laws before offering liquor upgrades. Some city rules will allow you to offer complimentary alcohol, but you cannot use it as an upgrade and charge for it.

If you want to offer your couples wine before their couples massage included it complimentary in the couples package. Check your city rules, as you do not want to violate the laws and be fined or shut down.

If you use snack and beverage upgrade create an attractive display. Presentation is everything. You can have bowl of fresh fruit. You can have basket of individually wrapped snacks like nuts or crackers.

You can have a dish of individually wrapped chocolates.

Some business will make special occasion snacks for example chocolate covered strawberries.

Snack and beverage upgrade package can be offered before or after their sessions.

Stretching upgrade is another popular upgrade.

Some therapist offer 10 minutes of stretching before the massage. The customer is fully clothed and the therapist can perform a variety of stretches before the session starts. Some bodyworkers offer stretching with body upgrades and have their clients select a muscle group for stretching during the session.

Another outside the box upgrade can include a coaching or a consultation. Some bodyworkers or energy workers work with nutrition, aromatherapy, and other products that assist with health and wellness. If you would like the opportunity to offer a consultation or assessment, use it as an upgrade.

The upgrade can be a mini session. If you are wanting to promote your products, you can run a free upgrade offer. For example, if you are selling nutrition products you can run a free nutrition consultation upgrade. This allows you to showcase other services, without pushy sales.

If you a coach, you can offer a mini coaching upgrade special. This will allow your clients to sample the service.

Remember upgrades not only bring in more money, they are also a soft way to introduce your other services and products. When clients see a list of your upgrades, they often discover new services or products they did not know were available. You are planting seeds. They might not sign up for the extra upgrade today, but you have planted seeds for those upgrade options.

A common story is a client who is not interested in the service or product, but they end up referring your business to a friend or coworker who benefits from one of your services or products.

Awareness and exposure are important when growing your business. You never know what connections and contacts your clients have. Offering upgrades and add ons is a soft way to share all the services you offer.

Upgrade Description and Pricing

Your upgrade description is extremely important. Here is your opportunity to showcase and highlight your upgrade offers. You want to take the time to write descriptions that will capture the interest of your clients.

You want to share the benefits of the upgrade. Remember the benefit can be for both the body and the mind. Often people will add on a service because it feels more decedent. Offer a variety of upgrades with different benefits to appeal to your wide range of customers.

You want to find a few powerful sentences for each upgrade description. If you are too wordy, many clients will not read. If it is too basic, clients will not be curious or attracted. Create your list of upgrades, then start to write descriptions for each one.

This creative process can take a few days as you keep fine tuning your ideas and words. Have friends and family read your descriptions. Ask them what they find appealing. What pulls their attention?

If you do not like writing descriptions hire someone to do it for you.

Writers have special talent to rearrange your words and create enticing attractive, appealing descriptions that sell.

You may not excel at writing and the art of selling with words. It might be smart to spend your time doing what you love, and hire someone to do the writing.

One mistake many single business owners make is trying to wear all the hats. Don't miss out on this huge financial opportunity because your writing skills are average.

Know when to get help. Resource people who specialize in product descriptions.

If you want to write the description yourself, write 2 or 3 different description for each upgrade, then ask friends and family their opinions.

If you do create your list of upgrades and they are not selling, you can rename them and re describe them.

How to price your upgrades? First of all, calculate the cost of the upgrades. If you are buying products, you want to include the cost of products in your upgrades.

You can also research businesses in your area to get an idea of going rate for upgrades.

Keep in mind, you are the creator of your upgrades.

You do not have to do same as other businesses.

I find the business research helps those individuals who tend to under sell their services.

Being aware what other businesses charge, can help individuals realize they are underpricing.

I have found businesses have more success if they charge on the high end. Customers subconsciously assume your business must be awesome if your clients are paying those prices.

Another idea to keep in mind, will you be running specials or promotions on your upgrades? If you will be strategically using upgrades for marketing, you will want the prices to be higher.

For example - if you have a 50% off promotion on upgrades, your upgrades will attract more attention.

If you underprice your upgrades, it will be a challenge to offer specials.

Remember marketing 101 tip, create an urgency.

If your Himalayan salt stone upgrade is only $10.00. There is no urgency to sign up today.

If that upgrade is regularly $15.00 or $20.00 and you have a 50% off upgrade sale, clients will be more likely to try it.

Some customers are motivated by getting a good deal. Customers want to feel they made a smart purchase. Sales and discounts help the budget customer feel they made a smart choice.

You can always change your prices, but keep in mind if clients see prices raising often, they can get irritated.

Sometimes it is better to over price, run specials and get clients acclimated. If clients see your upgrades are from $15.00 to $25.00 dollars, they will feel they are getting a great deal if you run a special. They will know the value of that upgrade is worth more.

Selling Upgrades

Selling upgrades is easy. One tool you see on cruise ships is the display platter. On their front desk, they have a physical display of the tools or products used on upgrades or specialty packages.

For example, they will have the bamboo massage tools displayed, the Himalayan salt stones, and the scented herbal Thai balls. Clients can touch the tools and smell the products.

This display is brilliant as the clients touch the tools, their mind automatically starts to image what the tool would feel like on their body. Getting a client to daydream about the upgrade is an easy way to sell your upgrades.

Another easy and simple way to sell your upgrades is to have laminated attractive flyers laying around your office and waiting areas. As customers are waiting, they will notice this attractive flyer and read all the upgrade options.

If you want to do a more direct approach, when a client checks in, you can hand the client the laminated flyer and ask as if she or he would like to add on any upgrades to their session.

There are a variety of ways to sell your upgrades depending on your style and personality.

You can also display your list of upgrades in an attractive frame and have displayed in your treatment rooms. This will plant seeds for future visits.

You can run promotions on all or certain upgrades. In your social media platforms, you can share an image of the upgrade, highlight a few of its benefits and share the special offer. You can do a percent off or a dollar amount off.

If the upgrade does not cost you any money, you can run a super low promotion on that upgrade. This can help you bring your clients to your website. Clients will discover all your upgrade options. They often discover services and products that peak their interest and they become curious. This plant seeds for future sales.

If you have a product that is about to expire, run a promotion on that upgrade. Don't let your products go to waste. Either offer a wonderful promotion on that upgrade or give it away complimentary. You can tell all your customers that week you are offering a complimentary peppermint sugar scrub (whatever the expiring product is). Give them to option to receive the complimentary gift. Clients are always dazzled when they are offered something for free.

This is a great way to create loyal customers as well as, therapists find their tips increase when giving clients a free upgrade.

You can use upgrades for birthday celebrations.

You can advertise and market your birthday clients receive a complimentary upgrade of their choice. Happy birthday to them from you. People love to celebrate birthdays with massage. Giving this birthday gift is a great way to honor your clients.

You can use upgrades as a thank you or as a customer service tool. Perhaps an unexpected issue happened on their visit, offer them a free upgrade. For example, if you are running behind and your client had to wait for you. You can apologize you are running behind and tell them you would like to offer them a complimentary upgrade during their session. This is fantastic customer service. Use your upgrades to prevent customers from becoming frustrated. Create raving fans with complimentary upgrades!

Marketing Upgrades to New Clients

When you have new clients come to your business, they usually fill out paperwork. On your paperwork, you can have a list of your popular upgrades. They can check if they want to add on one or more of the upgrades.

We find businesses who include this feature on their paperwork sell many upgrades. This paperwork also gives you the option to offer specials. If your paperwork has upgrades listed at $20.00 you can use a colored pen and cross out the $20.00 with an X and write SALE - 50% off. This is a great option, as you can decide each day and with each client if you want to offer them a discount.

Including a list of upgrades on your new customer paperwork has been very successful for all types of business.

Kathleen Thompson has a small practice with few employees. She was having a challenge implementing upgrades sales. She offered a bonus for each upgrade sale to give her staff incentive to sell.

Unfortunately, they were not selling. They changed their new client release form and added in a list of 6 popular upgrades. When her staff had a new client, she wrote discounts on their paperwork. With the 50% off written on the paperwork, customers would ask questions about the services. The staff started getting upgrade requests. The staff noticed how much clients liked the upgrades and they felt good about providing the service. Their paychecks started to increase.

Without working more, her staff started making more money from the upgrades. They started to feel the benefits of selling upgrades. Customers were very happy and her staff was happy. As her staff got more comfortable, they started asking their customers if they wanted an upgrade. They learned how to offer the upgrade directly as they began to believe in the value of the upgrades.

Taking the time to make a list of upgrades is a win win investment. You give your clients an opportunity to discover more favorite treatments.

Treatments benefit their body and rejuvenate their spirit. Upgrades allow your therapists the opportunity to switch up their sessions and earn more. Upgrades generate more money.

Thank you for clicking the Add On button and purchasing this book! It is my hope you Add On more success. Add On more new clients. Add On more loyal clients. Add On more fun at work. Add On more profits. Add On more joy and satisfaction with your career and business.

Ultimate Gift Card Sales & Marketing Secrets

5 Business Marketing Secrets To Selling More Gift Cards

Book 4

Sabrina Tonneson

Introduction

Gift cards are smart marketing. Gift cards are a cost-effective advertising tool. Gift cards increases sales. Gift cards improve brand awareness. Gift cards generate new customers. Gift cards keep loyal customers. It is easy to see the benefits of promoting and selling gift cards.

The question is, can you use the tool of gift cards to create more business? Can you double or triple your gift card sales? Can you create high gift card sales every month, not just during the holiday months?

This book uses samples for the spa and massage therapy industry. All service businesses will benefit from these secrets.

Secret #1 - Avoid Underpricing

A huge gift card mistake is underpricing. Some business owners feel the only way to sell high volume of gift cards is to offer a low-price gift card.

This thought or belief can hurt your business.

As a savvy business owner, you know you want to generate interest, you want to attract buyers to your gift cards.

Dropping prices is one way to attract buyers but what if there are other ways? Instead of assuming price is the one and only tool, let's think outside the box and create other ideas.

How can underpricing gift cards harm your business? One of the reoccurring things I witness with small business owners is their hunger to sell gift cards, then their frustration with redeeming those super low priced gift cards.

This cycle can loop a business into a negative pattern.

Businesses want the dollars today, but next week (or later) when it is time to provide the service, they lack the original enthusiasm.

Let me break it down for service businesses. The business owner drops the price. The bigger the price drop, the more they sell.

The owner gets financial relief when they receive the immediate dollars. A sense of security is experienced. Breathing room, now there is money to pay bills. Perhaps, even money to treat yourself to something.

Fast forward, many businesses have spent all the gift card sales money. Now clients are booking those gift card appointments. Therapist can work all day with customers who are redeeming their gift cards. Some therapists feel frustrated when they see another gift card client booked. When a therapist is frustrated or feeling worried about money, the quality of their service can change. Instead of seeing the gift card customer as a potential new regular client, they see the gift card customer as a pain in their elbow. (Massage humor never gets old.)

Keep in mind this is not how every business operates, this is not a fact for everyone. I want to bring awareness to the dangers of getting upside down financially and energetically.

A mistake an upside-down business can make is underpricing for more the gift cards.

They get a dollar today for a service tomorrow. This mindset can create more business discomfort.

If the business has already spent the gift card money, then when it is time to offer the body work, sometimes the therapist feels they are working for free.

Logically you know you are not working for free, but energetically you can feel you get no benefit when you giving an already spent gift card session. Bodywork is energetic. If you are feeling irritated or frustrated, it can be reflected in your performance. Yes, you may still give a good treatment, but will it be your best treatment?

When you have enthusiasm for your appointments, you naturally give high quality work.

You may think you are fooling your clients, as you have a smile on your face and you do not verbally share you are frustrated there will be no payment. Your clients may not understand or be aware of subtle energy. They may think to themselves, that was good session.... but I don't know if I will return, something was off. They leave not upset, but not a raving fan either.

If you want to underprice your gift cards, be mindful about why you are using that tool. You may want to keep your gift card sales income separate, this can avoid that feeling of working all day without getting paid. Create a system that allows you to keep your enthusiasm and sustains your excellent work ethic.

The secret to avoid underpricing is to create value to your services. Create packages that will allow you to increase the price of the service. We will go into detail on ways to create value later in the book. Once you have created packages with increased value, you offer your discounts from these higher price points. This will allow you to earn the same or more money per hour.

Secret #2 - Year-Round Sales

One gift card mistake is the belief that gift card sales are for the holidays. Many businesses miss out on huge gift card sales because they only promote gift cards during the holiday season. Realizing every month of the year, you can sell high volume of gift cards is a new thought to some individuals.

Don't miss more sales and more appointments because you failed or forget to promote gift cards every month.

Awareness of the gift card power will shift the amount of your gift card sales.

Imagine gift cards are your secret super power.

Don't put your gift cards back in the drawer after Christmas. Keep your super powers visible and in front of all your potential customers and existing customers.

Highlight and create gift cards promotions every month.

Occasions & Ideas:

Birthdays, Showers, Graduation, Thank you, Christmas, Valentines, Mother's Day, Father's Day, Weddings, Just Because, Staycation (Vacation At Home), 4th Of July, St Patrick's Day, National Massage Week, Spring Break, Halloween, Grandparent's Day, May The Force Be With You (May 4th) and more. Look at calendars for national holidays and daily celebration for more unique ideas.

Secret #3 - Terms

The secret sauce of gift card marketing is creating terms that benefit your business.

First, let's discuss gift card laws. Please research your state laws on gift card rules and guidelines.

A common law is the purchase price of the gift card never expires. Some people wonder why they need an expiration date on the gift card if the purchase price never expires.

Great question. If you are selling a service, the price of your service can change. For example, you can sell a 60-minute massage for $70.00 and you have it expire in one year.

If the customer wants to redeem that gift card 3 months after the expiration date, they can use the expired gift card, but its value is only for the purchase price.

If your current price for a 60-minute massage is $85.00, the customer will pay with the expired 60 minute massage gift card and pay an additional $15.00.

Having an expiration date on your gift cards is very important. This protects your business and encourages your customers to use their gift cards.

Gift cards can be sold in either dollar amount or services.

Businesses usually make a basic gift card certificate and will sell both service gift cards and dollar amount gift cards.

When selling a dollar amount, you can write 'never expires' on the expiration date line.

When using gift cards as a marketing tool you want to use the terms and expiration date to benefit your business. You will sell services and create packages that have high value. You will sell these high value packages at a discounted price. You can have the gift cards expire in 90 days or 6 months. You can have your regular price services expire in a year.

If a customer asks why it expires so soon, explain it is a promotion. If they want to pay full price they will have a year. This allows the customer to select and there is no pushy sales pitch from you.

The budget gift card shopper wants the best deal and they are willing to accept the terms in order to get the best deal.

Terms are key to creating successful gift card campaigns.

Create gift card campaigns that benefit your business. Use strategic planning to organize and prepare for your campaigns.

During your busy seasons, do not offer as big of a discount on your packages. During your slow season create offers that will keep you busy during your slow cycle.

For an example:

If you have a 3-month slow cycle - consider offering 2 sessions for X price or 3 sessions for X price. The secret will be the gift cards will expire in 3 months.

These gift cards can be used by same person or shared with others.

Customers see the great deal and they decide in advance to purchase.

If you sell your 60-minute massage for $75.00 - consider offering a 50-minute massage with hot stones for $79.00 or 2 for $129.00.

The package of 2, you will earn $65.00 for 50 minutes AND you will get 2 appointments during your slow season.

When clients are paying for the single session at $79.00 - you can tell them if they buy 2 it will only be $129.00.

Only $50.00 more for them to get a second massage. Of for an even better deal - have a 3 for $179.99

This will drop the price to $59.99 per 50-minute session. The price is lower but you are getting 3 appointments during the slow season. Give them the second and third massage in a gift card form. They can use gift cards themselves or give as a gift.

The secret will be the gift card will expire in 3 months. This promotion allows your customer to get a good value and it allows your business to get 2 or 3 appointments during your slow season.

This is an example of how the business can use the terms and expiration to benefit the business.

If the customer does not use the gift card within the term, the gift card price is still valid. If they bought the packages of 3, they paid $59.99 for each gift card. They can redeem an expired gift card and pay the additional cost of the now price.

If you are slow during certain days of the week or certain times you can customize specific gift card campaign.

For an example - Early Bird Gift Card Campaign.

You can offer great discounted packages during a specific window.

If you are getting specific with the terms, make sure your clients are aware these discounted gift cards can only be redeemed during the early bird hours.

One massage franchise advertised really low prices and sold a massive amount of gift cards at discounted price. The customers we unaware these discounted gift cards could only be redeemed from 8 am to 10 am or 8 pm to 10 pm. The business was not clear on their promotional advertisement. The business got a bad reputation as they upset many customers.

Possible new clients never gave that business a chance as they felt manipulated.

There are many budget customers who will be happy to prepay for discounted massages and they will love your early bird campaigns.

Some customers priority is savings; therefore, they are happy to schedule their appointments during the times they can save the most money.

Be clear on the terms and keep everyone on the same page. No one will feel your advertising tricked them.

Next, consider blackout dates. Valentine's week is often a super busy season. You can make this week a blackout week.

If you are going to have blackout dates, make sure they are clear on the gift cards and on your marketing promotional tools, like your website and flyers.

If you run a January promotion campaign, some clients may purchase the gift cards planning to use the deals for Valentine's week. It is important to have all your terms easy to see and read, this will prevent any frustration.

All sale final. This is an important term to consider including on your gift cards. Occasionally you will get a person who wants to return or get a refund on a gift card. Prevent any possible hassles with clear gift card rules and guidelines.

Secret #4 - The Magic of Buy 1, Get 1

Gift card sales will dramatically increase with this Buy 1, Get 1 strategy.

Most businesses do not use the superpower of the Buy 1, Get 1 because they assume they will lose money.

Buy 1, Get 1 can be used in 3 different ways.

1. Buy 1 and get a second one of equal value.

2. Buy 1 and get a second one of a different value or package.

3. Buy 1 and get a bonus gift card for _____ dollar amount.

People love BOGO or Buy 1, Get 1 because BOGO benefits the buyer. The buyer gives the gift card and then keeps the second offer for themselves.

We see many BOGO offers during the holiday season.

Restaurants often participate in BOGO.

Cheesecake Factory created a brilliant holiday gift card campaign with their BOGO offer. For every gift card they sell, they give a FREE slice of cheesecake gift card.

This is brilliant as they are known for their famous cheesecake.

They make money from this promotion because they use the secret marketing tool of terms. This free slice of cheesecake has a specific time window to be redeemed.

It cannot be redeemed on the day of the gift card purchase. It is redeemed after the holidays. This is brilliant as many people dine out extra during the month of December than they tend to stay home in January.

Their BOGO offer can only be redeemed in the beginning of the new year until March, this helps keep their business booming.

The slice of cheesecake has a value of about $10.00, but the cost of the cheesecake does not cost the business $10.00. Instead of giving away $10.00 gift card with every gift card purchase, they make more profit by offering the free slice of cheesecake. Their slice of cheesecake has a very high markup price.

Many restaurants will give away a bonus $10.00- or $20.00-dollar gift card for orders over $50.00 or $100.00. They also use the secret tool of terms to benefit them. They only allow the bonus gift card to be used during certain dates.

Use the magic of the Buy 1, Get 1 to benefit your business.

You will get the most sales from the Buy 1, get the exact same 1 FREE offer.

If your 60-minute massage is 80.00 and you offer buy one get 1 free, you would only receive $40.00 per massage. Businesses assume the loss is too high, therefore, they don't use the magic of Buy 1, Get 1 Free.

How can we use the magic of Buy 1, Get 1 to sell gift cards and make money?

Outside the box marketing will help us create ideas.

In my popular Massage Marketing Books - Volume 1, I share many ways to earn more money without working more hours. The secret is to create packages that have more value and this allows you to charge more.

Instead of focusing on the basic 75-minute massage, let's focus on a 75-minute package. Your package can include dry brushing, full body massage with Himalayan salt stones, aromatherapy scalp massage and hot towel peppermint foot wrap. This package you have included 4 extra upgrades. You will charge more for this package, even though it will not take you more hands on time. Instead of $90.00 for a basic 75-minute massage you can charge $179.00 for the package packed with upgrades.

Create a catchy name and write an attractive description for your package. For packaging ideas, check out my book, <u>Don't Leave Money On The Table</u>.

Showcase the benefits of the therapy enhancements and use words that sell the experience.

If you offer a buy one, get 1 free you will be earning the same price. You will have a small investment in the equipment and products. Wash and disinfect the equipment and you can use your tools over and over again. Products can only be used one time obviously. A bottle of peppermint essential oil can be sprinkled on your hot towels and used on multiple clients. Select upgrades that are cost effective for you.

If you want to make money with your Buy 1, Get 1, change the Get 1. Your Get 1, does not have to be the exact same offer. Your Get 1 can be a different package.

If you want to sell a gift card at a lower price point, here is an idea. If your 60-minute price is $70.00.

Create a 60-minute package with therapy enhancements upgrades. Sell package for $99.99.

If you want to offer a Buy 1, Get 1 - your Get 1 can be a 30-minute package.

You can create a 30-minute massage express package or a 30-minute foot treatment package.

In this case scenario you will receive $29.99 for your 30-minute package.

Buy 1, Get 1 can also be a promotional gift card for a dollar amount. For example, you may sell your 99.00 package and the Get 1, can be a promotional $20.00 gift card. Customers can give this $20.00 gift card to the person they are buying the gift for, or they can keep and use themselves.

Decide terms on your promotional gift cards. Be clear on the terms. Write dates that promotional gift cards can be redeemed.

For example: Promotional Gift Cards can be redeemed June 1 to June 30th 2018.

When designing your Promotional Gift Cards, you can have a blank line printed. Then any month you offer a promotional gift card you can write in the redeeming dates.

Make sure to write 'Promotional Gift' on your gift card. If you live in a state where gift card never expires, your promotional gift cards can expire. The reason they can expire is because the buyer does not purchase these gift cards. These gift cards are promotional offers from the business.

Decide how many gift cards you want to sell each month then decide which type of Buy 1, Get 1 will be most effective to reach your goal.

Secret #5 – Semi-Annual Gift Card Campaign

One secret only a few businesses have tapped into in the Semi-Annual sale. This sale will be a big sale. It will be similar to your Black Friday sale.

Businesses can master these 2 big sales and be set for the whole year.

Take the time to create a business marketing strategy for your big Semi-Annual sale. One of the benefits of the mid-year sales is not sharing the gift cards promotions with other businesses. During the Black Friday campaign, you are among many businesses running specials and promotions. The Semi-Annual gift card campaign is not popular and most businesses miss this huge opportunity.

One way to make this campaign a huge success is get the buzz going before the campaign starts.

In your email blasts and social media posts start talking about the Semi-Annual Gift Card Campaign.

Tease your audience with some information. Wet their appetite so they become curious and interested in what you are going to offer.

Create your best deals two times a year during these big promotions. The first time you run this big sale your customers might miss out as they make the mistake of assuming the special sale will not expire. When they see the prices are higher the following week, they will not make the mistake of missing out on the next big sale.

Use the terms to benefit your business. I suggest a 3 to 6-month expiration date.

This is one reason it is important not to blur the marketing campaigns. If you offer same big sale and discounts each month, your clients will not take your two big sales seriously.

I suggest your big Semi-Annual sale be for one week only. Let your audience know the exact dates the gift card sale will be. Many people are busy and they think they will buy later and they forget to buy. Create that urgency with a short-term sale.

Prep for the sale two or three weeks in advance. Plan to be busy preparing for the sale. If you do not like marketing and promoting, hire someone. Hire someone to do your social media promotions. Many people will freelance and do all your online promotions.

Send out posts and blasts before the sale to generate interest. Every day during the campaign send out daily posts. Create flyers and pass out to local businesses. Hire someone to distribute your flyers.

If you have small operation, you can offer an open house for your gift card sales. In your promotional advertisement, let your clients know the time you will be open for gift card sales. Offer complimentary beverages and snacks during open house. Have samples of the products they will be receiving in the treatments. Have warm stones available for them to touch and feel. Have aromatherapy lotions and scents for them to sample. If you are offering jade roller face massage, have the jade rollers available for them to feel. Use the products and scents to help your clients image the treatment. This will help you sell even more gift cards.

Make sure your online gift card sales platforms have accurate prices and match your big promotional offers.

Avoid over selling gift cards. You may wonder what is the harm in over selling? If you are a one-person operation and you already have a steady stream of regulars and you over sell gift cards, your clients will have a hard time scheduling. If you have a 1 month or more waiting list, limit how many gift cards you sell.

On your marketing promotions, include how many gift card sales you are selling. This will let your customers know there is a limit. Clients will appreciate if you do not over sell, as customers can get frustrated if they are never able to book their appointments.

This is also fantastic marketing, as it sends the message to your clients you are busy. Clients like working with someone who is busy. They like knowing others find your services as fabulous as they find your services. It helps them appreciate you and appreciate their time on your table.

Do all the prep work so your big sales week flows by with ease and grace.

Keep track of the sales and the results. This will help you fine tune your next campaign. You will get clear on what works, what is popular with your clients and what works with your business. If you run into challenges, that is ok too. Often, we discover how to succeed when we create a flop or a failure. It all helps to create the success and type of business that works best for you.

Gift cards are wonderful tool to grow your business. Clients will look forward to seeing what creative offers you are selling each month. Monthly gift card campaigns can help you keep your services fresh and interesting.

You can experiment and try new services. Give your business the gift of receiving prepaid sessions. Give your business the gift of having financial security. Give your business the gift of creative and innovative business building ideas.

My bonus gift to you is a complimentary book.

I have included my book, <u>Double Your Holiday Gift Card Sales</u>. This book will help you market your gift cards. Jumpstart your monthly gift card sales volume by using the marketing ideas throughout the year.

Double Your Holiday Gift Card Sales

Sell More Gift Certificates Without Under Pricing

Bonus Book

Sabrina Tonneson

Black Friday Deals

Black Friday is an American shopping celebration. It is an invitation to spend money buying gifts, products and services for others and yourself. Black Friday is a wonderful opportunity for all businesses.

Take the time to create a Black Friday campaign and take advantage of this wonderful opportunity to attract new clients and get prepaid massages.

I suggest your Black Friday campaign be different than your December campaign.

Typically, Black Friday is the one time of the year customers can receive your best deals. If you run a promotion for Black Friday and then you continue to use the same offer in December it will teach your customers there is no urgency or reason to buy in November. Your customers will lose trust in your advertising promotions.

I find businesses who run a Black Friday offer and then they continue to offer same promotion in December irritating. Why did I purchase in November when I could have done my shopping in December? I feel the business tricked me and it leaves a bad taste in my mouth.

Create strong relationships with your customers by creating a December Holiday campaign and a different Black Friday campaign.

One mistake many businesses make with holiday sales promotions is underpricing. How can you avoid this mistake?

First of all, become aware that a promotion does not have to equal low discounted prices. You can create value to your services without losing money. Use smart marketing to create value to your services.

One smart way to create value to your service is to create a package. Instead of selling a basic 60-minute massage service, sell a 60-minute massage package. When you create packages, you can add in value which will increase the price.

Your packages can include therapy enhancement upgrades. Your package can include complimentary beverage, snacks or chocolate. Your packages can include products. Your packages can include guided meditations or visualizations.

There are many ways to create packages and offer more than the basic massage service. When you create these packages, you can charge more. You can strategically price these packages and create eye catching specials.

For example: Your 90-minute massage is $100.00.

You can create an Ultimate Relaxation Package.

This package can include aromatherapy scalp massage, deep relaxing hot stones and peppermint hot towel foot treatment. Customers are given their choice of complimentary tea, apple cider or hot chocolate with a snack size bag of almonds or peanuts.

This package can sell for $199.00

Now you can run a fabulous promotion for this package.

Black Friday Deal, you offer Buy 1, Get 1 FREE.

In December, you can change the offer to

Buy 2, Get 1 FREE.

Black Friday Deals you will earn your basic $100 per session and your December promotions you would earn $133 per session. You do not spend more time on the package, you have a slight investment with the upgrades. Once you have purchased the hot stones and equipment you have no more investment. The cost for the aromatherapy, beverage and snacks is less than $2.00 per package.

With these great Black Friday Deals you can have the expiration date sooner. If you usually have a 12-month term for expiration, I suggest you offer a 6-month term for expiration. Remember the purchase price never expires. If a customer does not come in for a year, they will receive the purchase price of the expired gift card and they will pay the additional cost of the service.

Clients want to receive a deal. Our culture has taught us to take pride in finding deals. We brag to our friends when we discover a great deal. We feel happy investing our dollars when we feel we manifested a great deal.

Allow your customers to feel great by creating great deals for them!

You can start your Black Friday promotions anytime in November. You can add a page to your website showing what your Black Friday Deals will be. You can include a sneak peek to Black Friday Deals in your email blasts and social media. Let your customers know this is your BEST offer. Your offer will expire at end of November.

Decide the time line you will sell your Black Friday Promotions. I suggest start on Black Friday (the day after Thanksgiving) and run promotion to the end of the month. Make it as easy as possible for your clients to purchase their gift cards. If you only sell your packages at your business location, set up days and times for your customers to come in and purchase.

Offer A Variety of Packages

A smart marketing tool is to create a variety of packages. You will attract more clients and sell more gift cards if you have a variety of options available for your customers.

There are many different types of consumers searching for deals. One consumer might be looking for a gift for a daycare provider or a teacher. One consumer might be looking for a gift for a boss or coworker. One consumer might be looking for a gift for family member or partner.

You can image these 3 different kinds of consumers have different prices they want to spend. Most people will invest more on a gift for a partner than for a teacher.

In order to appeal to all these types of consumers, create a variety of offers with different prices.

One way to keep the prices low is offer a package that is only 30 minutes or 45 minutes. If you are investing less time on the service you can lower the price.

I suggest you sell 3 types of packages. Low, medium and high price points packages.

Here is a list of different package ideas.

Rejuvenate Package

Enjoy a 30-minute foot treatment with warm relaxing hot stones and hot towels.

Serenity Package

Drift away with a 45-minute massage package. Package includes soothing face and scalp massage. Optional hot oils scalp treatment included.

Release your stress with neck shoulder and back massage.

Relaxation Package

Bring your body back to balance with a calming 60-minute full body massage. Package includes warm relaxing hot stones and your choice of aromatherapy.

Tranquility Package

Fall into a deep state of peace and tranquility with this wonderful 90-minute full body massage. This package includes lavender infused hand and foot treatment, relaxing salt stones, hot towels and calming face massage with hot & cold stone face treatment.

The Royal Treatment Package

Give yourself the decedent experience of a 2-hour session. You will select your choice of 3 body treatments. Customize your appointment to include all your favorites. (Write a list of the treatments you offer)

Remember to have an expiration on all your gift cards. Check with your state to see what is your state regulated rules on gift card sales. In my state, if a gift card is sold at a promotional value and it expires, the amount paid for the gift card never expires, however the customer would pay the cost difference of the now prices.

For example, if you sold a 60-minute massage for $75.00 two years ago. Today the customer wants to come in and use the expired gift card. Your current price for a 60-minute massage is $100.00. The customer would turn in the hard copy gift card and pay the additional $25.00.

Strategic Ways to Get New Customers

Give away free gift certificates. First create your gift cards. You can create gift cards online. Google 'gift card templates' and fill in the template and print.

I like to order gift cards from vistaprint dot com.

I design my own gift cards on their postcards.

The front of the postcard I use an image of massage therapy. The back side I have a soft black and white image with my information printed on top.

I include:

To: _____   From: _____

(If you are giving away the free gift write your business name on the 'From' line. This allows you to have the dollar amount expire, as your business gave this gift certificate as a free promotional offer.)

A blank line for the offer _____

Smaller font, I include my business name, address, telephone number and website.

I include a Number ____.

This allows me to write a number for each gift card in order to keep track of them

Expiration _____.

If you have any blackout dates, or specific guidelines include on the bottom in smaller font.

For example:

Gift cards not valid the week of Valentine's. All Sales Final

Another option is go to a stationery store and purchase gift certificates already printed.

Make sure you fill out the gift cards with your business contact information.

Include an expiration date!

This is a terrific way to get new clients and make money. You are going to give away a free gift to people. You are going to pass out promotional gift certificates.

It can range from $10 to $30 dollars. If you want to grow your business quickly offer a higher dollar amount.

The MOST important piece of this marketing strategy is to include on promotional gift card,

'One gift card promotion per person.'

If you are not allowing people to use promotional gift cards for gift certificates, include that information on your gift cards.

'Gift card promotions not valid for gift certificate purchases.'

It will depend on your business and your holiday promotions. If you are going to allow the gift card to be used on holiday promotion, pass out your holiday flyer with your promotional gift certificates.

You want to pass out these gift cards to new people. One idea is to partner with other businesses. If you know someone who is a business owner and they are giving their clients a Christmas gift, they can include your gift certificate.

For example, if you know someone who is a stylist and they give away holiday presents to their regular clients, they can include your gift card. Their customers will love it. If this business person has free gifts for you to give your clients, you can exchange.

It is a smart marketing arrangement even if the other businesses provide no gift for your clients. You are getting an opportunity to develop a relationship with new customers.

You can give these gifts to neighboring businesses. This is a great way to market your business. People love to find a massage therapist close to their work.

You can go to neighbor businesses - regardless if they are retail, offices, factories, etc and gift them your free gift cards.

You can say something like. Hello! My name is _____ from _____. (You can mention you are neighbors)

I wanted to take a moment to wish you a happy holiday season as well as to leave you a little gift. (If it is a big business with many employees you can share several gift cards) I have some free gift certificates for you to share with your staff or employees. Thank you! Happy holidays.

Leave your holiday gift card flyers if they can use the gift certificates on gift card purchases. It will be easy and convenient holiday shopping for the people who work near your business.

You can also drive to other businesses in your city or town and pass out your information. Go door to door and walk into all types of business.

You can do this anytime of the year. Have a few flyers or promotional materials. Hand them to person who is sitting at the front desk. You can say something like this.

Hello - I am passing out free coupons. You can pass them out or leave in your breakroom. Thanks.

It is that simple. No one will say you cannot leave a free coupon or flyer. You are not taking up their time. You are popping in with a smile on your face and leaving a flyer. You never know who will see your promotional flyers or gift certificates.

If you have more time than you have advertising dollars, go around your city and stop into local businesses. Many business owners grow their businesses quickly with the simple tool of investing one hour a week visiting businesses with their flyers or promotions.

Some businesses will start to depend on your monthly promotional items and look forward to seeing you. Some businesses may inquire about on-site chair massage. The possibilities are endless when you are willing to take some of your time and help people become aware of your business.

Sell Gift Certificates Online

One of the best ways to sell your gift certificates is instantly with online gift sales. One company I recommend is called gift certificate cafe. This company charges a one-time setup fee, approximately $50.00

It is an easy process. They will send you links you can use on your websites and social media. These links will allow customers to instantly receive a gift card. The company will collect the information, send the email gift card and they have an easy tracking system for you use.

The charge 5% of each gift card sale, plus the credit card charges.

If you sell hundreds of dollars each month you can sign up for a different plan.

Some businesses don't want to pay out so much in fees.

I suggest you invest in the company and increase your prices to cover their fees.

The reason I feel it is worth the investment is because many people are last minute shoppers. Last minute shoppers are not worried about prices. Last minute shoppers want convenience.

The site allows you to sell a specific dollar amount or a package. I suggest you use both. The site also allows you to run specials and promotions. They have a great system and I feel they are worth the price.

Another idea is to also sell gift cards via US mail. You can sell these gift cards at lower prices as you will not have to pay the additional 5% fee.

Your website can have US mail gift cards and Instant gift cards. The budget conscious shopper is going to order gift cards in advance and avoid the higher prices.

If you do not have a shopping cart on your website, it is easy to use PayPal.

Sign up with PayPal. It is a free service. Once you have an account with PayPal, you can create buttons. These buttons are under the tool section. If you are confused call PayPal customer service and they will walk you through how to set up PayPal shopping on your website.

You will create your packages and flat rate dollar amounts on your website. Then add the PayPal buttons. PayPal will collect the money and charge you basic credit card fees. You will be responsible to mail out the gift cards.

If this is overwhelming, hire a freelancer to set up your online gift card sales. There is a huge audience who purchase online gift cards. Family and friends are going to purchase from the businesses that make online shopping easy.

Sell More Gift Cards At Your Business Location

First of all, you want to showcase your gift card specials. Create a flyer or hire someone to make a flyer for you. This will be an attractive flyer which will showcase your holiday promotions.

Frame this flyer or display this flyer in a location your customer will easily see. If you have a bigger business, I suggest you laminate a couple of these flyers. This will allow you to pass out to several people who are walk ins wanting to know your prices and services.

You want your flyer to be catchy with word choices that appeal to the senses. You will want to share what the regular price of the service. When customers see the service is $99.00 on special for $79.00, it helps them feel good about the purchase.

Create attractive gift card bags and boxes. These gift card bags displayed around your office plants the gift card sale idea to your customers.

You can include items in your gift card bags or boxes that create value. A king size candy bar is big in size, but small in price. An attractive gift bag, with matching tissue and a large candy inside looks more appealing than a gift card in a white envelope. People like opening a gift more than opening an envelope.

If you want to create gift boxes or baskets with products, you can showcase all the items with clear transparent wrapping, that allows customer to see all the products. Some businesses invest in candles, sea salts, chocolate, lotions, etc. and they create a gift basket. The downside can be if you buy more products than you sell. I suggest start with a smaller investment in products and if the gift baskets are really popular, buy more. You may not get as good a deal with a smaller order, but at least you won't waste money on products you do not sell.

A strategic marketing tool can be to have a big beautiful gift basket with a high-end price. Also, display smaller gift packages with lower prices. Customers see the high price tag, then all of sudden the lower price bag seems like a great deal. Other types of consumers want the best package and they will purchase your luxury basket.

25 Countdown Days - Social Media Engagement

Use the 25 days to Christmas as an opportunity to develop a connection with your social media audience. It is easy for specific period of time to commit to your social media marketing.

Each day post on your social media and include hashtag with the countdown and your business name.

You can create a variety of posts. The obvious post is the holiday massage photo. You can also rotate in inspirational quotes or feel good stories. Massage humor pictures are popular.

A great way to get in the habit of posting more on your social media it the goal of the 25 days countdown challenge. Challenge yourself to take a few minutes every day to post and engage with your social media followers. This is a great way to attract new followers and use the tool of social media to help market your business.

Some of the social media sites allow you to schedule the post in advance. If you feel you cannot do social media daily, create all 7 posts at one time and schedule them to post daily. Once a week posting might be an easier option for some of you.

I find the people who do not post on social media feel it is too complicated. It is actually very easy. Pick one or two social media platforms and start.

I highly recommend Facebook as one platform. A secret gem with Facebook business pages, is the search engines. Once you have a Facebook business page and over 25 likes, Facebook will put your business page in the search engines and new people can discover your business. It is a great FREE tool to attract new clients.

Happy Holidays! I look forward to hearing your success stories.

If you would like me to take a few minutes to review your holiday flyers or holiday promotions, you can contact me via email. SabrinaTonneson@gmail.com

Massage Marketing - Sorry We're Booked

Book 5

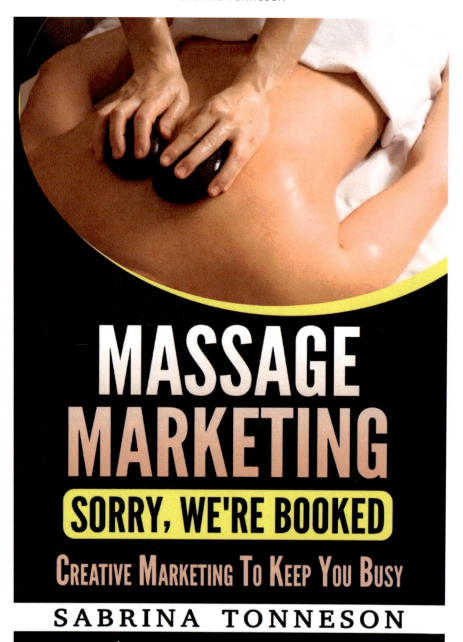

Introduction

How often do you hear massage therapists, bodyworkers or energy healers brag about their consistent income and their high paying career? Is it possible to have it all?

A job you love and an income that exceeds your expectations.

Sometimes people believe you either have a job you love or an income you love. That point of view can limit what is possible and what we can create. Over the years I have seen more and more people in the health and wellness industry find fulfillment in their careers and their income. More and more individuals are breaking through the limited beliefs about massage therapy income or alternative medicine income. I believe we can continue to break through more layers of limiting beliefs and we can create the career and income we want.

The journey to get you to your destination might have some bumps or challenges, therefore, it is important to keep in mind your destination. Keep daydreaming about the destination.

Imagine traveling, perhaps you have always wanted to go to Europe, but the airplane there can take over 10 hours. It can be a long uncomfortable ride, but once you arrive at the destination, you feel so happy you made the choice.

Or what if your dream destination is even further away, pretend you want to go to New Zealand. That journey can be a 20 plus hour airplane and layover experience.

The point is when we keep in mind why we are in the industry and where we are headed, it can help us sustain the enthusiasm and be committed to follow through.

I have done massage mentoring over the years. It was a free service. In the program, I would commit to work with individuals for 6 weeks. First, I found out what the therapist or bodyworker wanted to achieve. Then, we broke it into goals and created small weekly goals. The weekly goals were not time consuming, usually less than 2 hours of marketing and paperwork a week. I tried to teach individuals to get in the habit of setting small goals and having consistent follow through. I find many people start super strong, fiery hot, committed and determined. The first 2 weeks they achieved their weekly goals. By week 3, I usually noticed a change. Follow through started to decrease. Over the next few weeks the person getting the free mentoring starts to disappear.

I confess, I found it shocking.

I learned to see patterns of the individuals ready to create success. It is easy to say you want success. Words are free. Actions and behaviors support if you are congruent with your beliefs. If they were able to commit to themselves for those 6 weeks, I knew they were ready for success. Over the years I have been able to witness the joy and success individuals have created with their careers and businesses.

I would say the majority of the people I mentored quit. I would guess about 80% quit. It reminds me of something I heard a business coach share.

Over 90% of people who buy a book will quit reading after the first few chapters. Those who finish the book, only 5% of the people will implement or apply the wisdom from the book. (If you finish reading this book and you apply any of the ideas - Congratulations you are in a unique category.)

We live in a time of gathering information. It is fun and interesting to gather information. It can also be a type of trap. Investing time and money in books, seminars, webinars can be great, but learning without application will not change your income or your business.

I hope you, the reader, will find benefit from the ideas inside this book. I hope you will find a way to keep your enthusiasm strong and stay committed to follow through.

If you decide to invest 2 hours a week on marketing, you will get results. Imagine what the results will look like in 90 days! Are you willing to consistently invest 2 hours a week on your marketing?

It is my wish for you, that you will continue to daydream about your desired destination. If the ride feels uncomfortable or too long, I hope you stay committed to yourself, your vision, and the business you want to create. You will be proud of yourself when you arrive at destination.

Book Your Slow Days

Instead of sitting around waiting for clients to book appointments use smart marketing to fill your slow days. This is a guaranteed way to get clients and earn money.

Create a Drawing for FREE Massage

This drawing is going to benefit your business in many ways. First, everyone who enters to win a free massage, is a person who enjoys bodywork. A person who does not like massage therapy will not enter. The drawing is your way of attracting your target audience.

The people who enter the drawing will provide their name, email address and phone number.

This information is valuable as it will allow you to grow your database and your email lists.

How do you announce your drawing?

Social Media is an easy, free way to advertise your drawing. To do this successfully, create a visual image of massage with the words "FREE Massage". Remember this: "a picture is worth 1,000 words".

This word "FREE" will capture interest and curiosity.

You can have people who see your promotion on social media send you their contact information.

Another way to announce your promotion is to create a box or jar that lets people put their contact information inside. Create a cute box or jar. Have small pieces of paper available for them to fill out.

On the piece of paper type:

Name

Telephone

Email

Type this several times on a piece of paper and then cut out the pieces. Place these pieces of paper along with pens by your container.

Next, go to local businesses and ask if you can leave your free drawing at their front desks or break room. You may want to gift the business with a free massage as a thank you for allowing you to leave your attractive container at their location.

If you have connections with anyone who owns a business or has access to making business decisions, see if they will allow you to put your drawing at their work site.

You can place your drawings anywhere there are people; coffee shops, gas stations, beauty salons, factories, banks, or corporate businesses. Any location that has access to people.

The more places, the better, as this will widen your possibilities to attract different types of customers.

How do you make money with a FREE drawing?

Great question.

First, realize that if you are gifting a customer with your services, you get to decide the regulations.

If Tuesdays are your slow days, you will redeem the free massage on Tuesdays.

When you contact the winners, be sure to include the guidelines for redeeming the free gift.

I would suggest your free massage be a free 30-minute massage. When you are contacting the winners, you can offer an upsell. If they would like to upgrade to 60 minutes the price is _____.

You get to create the upgrade offer and the upgrade price.

Here is a sample of what you can say to the winners. You can call, text or contact them via email.

Congratulations _____ (name of winner)

You won a free massage! Your free massage can be redeemed this Tuesday or next Tuesday.

(Include dates or times here. If you have many openings in one week, you may extend your offer availability period. Monday - Wednesday from 9am to 2pm. Again, pick the dates and times that work best for you.)

If you would like to upgrade your session, we do have a few options available for you.

Add an additional 30 minutes for ___ (name the price).

Add on Himalayan Salt Stones for _____ (name the price)

The benefit of showing 2 or 3 add on options allows this person to customize their session. Maybe someone always wanted to try

Himalayan Salt Stones or Massage Cupping and the add on price is only $5.00. This would be perfect time to try it. Maybe someone enjoys 60 or 90-minute massage, this add on would be ideal for them.

Create upgrades that work for you. You can create anything you want.

If you are unable to come in during this time slot, you may share this gift with a friend, family member or co-worker who enjoys bodywork.

If you do not feel comfortable sharing the upgrade offer, you can include upgrades on your paperwork when they arrive.

When the winning person comes to your business to receive free massage, they will fill out paperwork. On the paperwork you have a list of upgrades and prices.

For example, you can offer hot stone upgrade for additional $5.00 or $10.00. Many of your free customers will pay for an upgrade. To learn more how to sell upgrades like hot stones, bamboo therapy, massage cupping, etc., please check out my book called <u>Add On The Serenity - Create Popular Upgrades That Sell.</u>

If you collect tips, this is going to be a great time to receive big tips. People are especially generous after receiving a free massage. If you want to encourage higher tips, have a tasteful tip jar in your massage room. You can use suggestive sales to encourage tips. An example would be to place 2 - $10.00 bills in your tip glass or a $20.00 bill.

Initially, when you are filling up your slow times, you may want to offer upgrades at lower prices. As your times are filling up, you can increase your upgrade prices.

You can customize each giveaway.

As you get busier and busier, continue to use your drawing to get new customers. In the beginning, you may give away 8 sessions a week, then as you get busier you might only give away one session a week.

You want to contact everyone who enters your drawing. Each person who enters is a prospective new client.

Send everyone an email or text.

Here is a sample idea on what to share:

Thank you for entering our free massage drawing. Unfortunately, you did not win a free massage. We appreciate you took your time to enter, as a thank you, we have a small gift for you.

Then create a gift for them. One fabulous gift idea is a gift card. Gift them a $10.00 to $25.00 gift card from your business. A gift card is similar to a coupon, but a gift card feels more important and valuable. If they have a $20.00 gift card, you will take $20.00 off the price of service.

In the beginning, if you are trying to grow your business quickly your gift cards might be a larger amount.

Remember to attach an expiration period to your gift. Expirations help motivate people to come in and receive their gift while your offer lasts. You are willing to gift away great gifts because you want to fill your books.

In a few months your books will be getting full and you will not want to be discounting the services so much. I would have gift card expire in 30 days to 60 days, depending on quickly you want to grow your business.

Important to know when giving away free gift card with a dollar amount, please make sure to include somewhere on the gift card, 'Promotional Gift Card'. This is important as in some states the dollar amount of the gift card never expires. This will protect your business, if a customer tries to use your promotional gift card in 2 years. Promotions that are given away free can legally expire.

Showcase Your Services with a Photo Testimony

The average consumer will look at your ads for 3 to 5 seconds. Count to 3. That is how much time you have to showcase your services. One powerful marketing tool businesses employ to arouse the interest of potential customers are photos. There is a reason they say a picture is worth 1,000 words. One fabulously designed visual image can generate a whole lot of interest.

Design a photo with an attached testimony. This helps potential customers see what services you are promoting. They can also read what customers are saying about your business. This will go a long way in helping potential customers choose your business.

Reviews are important to all businesses. If your business has an excellent reputation, use that asset to market your business.

After creating your testimony photo, share it on your social media pages. Share it on your newsletters and email blasts. Display your reviews on your website.

Making a testimonial review is easy: find a photo that showcases the service you want to promote. For instance, if you want to promote couples massage, use a couples massage photo.

There are free and paying websites that allow you to include text on your photos. Do a Google search with the phrase, 'add text to my picture'.

I use picmonkey dot com. This site was free, now there is a monthly charge of $3.00.

It can take a minute to learn how to operate the software on the website. If you have no patience, hire someone to create photo testimonies for you.

When creating your photo review, you want to make the words easy to read.

It is a great idea to add stars. A photo with 5 stars automatically indicates a fantastic review. If a person does not read the written review, they will instantly notice the 5 stars.

You can quote the full name of the person who left the review, with their permission. If they left you a review publicly online, use the name they signed, as some people only leave their first name or initials.

Texting Promotions

There are free websites that will send out texts for your business. This is a great tool to fill up your slow days. If you wake up one morning and you have no appointments scheduled, offer a last minute "text special" campaign.

Text specials will draw in last minute appointments.

Beware not to over-send text specials. How can you keep a balance and not make the mistake of over sending discounted specials?

First, start collecting text customers. You can do this by having a link on your website.

EZ Texting dot com is a free site. You are allowed to send 500 texts each month FREE.

They have a link that you can add to your website to collect numbers.

At your business location, you can have a signup sheet to collect text numbers.

You can also have it written on the release form. When new clients come in, they will fill out paperwork. You can add the question. Would you like to receive last minute text specials? (No more than one text per month).

You can organize the numbers you collect into groups of 50. This way you can rotate the text specials and target people at different times. If you have 100 numbers, you may decide to send out text offer to one group of 50 during one slow week. A few weeks later if you have another slow week, you can send out a text special to the next group of 50.

One mistake business make is over sending discounted prices. You do not want to give your clients the impression that you always offer specials so they never have to pay regular prices.

When you send out your text, include the link to your online booking. It is important to make scheduling an appointment as easy and convenient as possible. Most people do not like to call and wait on telephone to book an appointment.

Get OTHERS to Promote You

Let others do the work for you. Let others do the advertising for you.

You may think this is too good to be true. The truth is, it is actually really easy to let others market for you.

Think of people you know who love to talk, people who are very social. Social people love chatting. It is their natural state.

Write a list of people you know like this. Include on this list, people you know who have access to many people daily, a hair stylist for example.

Make a business arrangement with them. First, offer them a free massage. If they love your style and they are a raving fan, then ask them if they would like to create a business arrangement with you.

Give these people your promotional cards. Have business cards made with your promotional offering. Perhaps your New Customer offer or your special signature massage package (do not forget the expiration date).

Ask your raving fan to pass out your business promotion in exchange for one massage a month. You can ask them to do it for one or two months. This gives you an opportunity to see if you are getting results. Let them know it is temporary project. This is important, as someone may not do their part of the agreed business promoting, but they still expect to get their complimentary massage.

A smart way of tracking the results is by having each set of promotional cards have a special code. For example, if you give Mary 50 promotional business cards - write a little M on the back of these cards or a number. This will allow you to see where the promotional offers are coming from.

The great thing about partnering with people who use your services is they will be authentic with their recommendations. They will be genuine when they talk about your services. The best way to grow your business is through the application of personal recommendations.

Teach A Class

Use the tool of teaching to promote your business. This is a great way to create awareness about your industry and business. You can keep this very simple.

If you feel nervous or awkward, think about inviting others to join you. Write a list of people who could compliment your health and wellness classes. Some ideas are a reflexologist, a lymphatic practitioner, an energy healer, a Rolfer, aromatherapist, nutritionist, and a cranial sacral expert.

This could be a great way to add content to your classes as well as cross-promote with other business owners.

You can include some hands-on work during a class. If you are running a class on how to use reflexology to help with headaches or insomnia, you can bring in different lotions and have your audiences' practice on each other. Sounds interesting, right?

If you start to offer classes, the attendance will grow. Yes, people will start to look forward to your classes. It will help people get to know you. One of the best tools to get clients and keep them is to develop a relationship with them. During a class, you have an opportunity to connect with them on a more personal level. Be careful not to cross the line of being too personal and not professional, unless you want to become good friends with your customers.

If you find you enjoy teaching classes, you can contact your local community education office. You can offer to teach for them. They do the advertising and promotion for their Community Ed classes. This is a great way to raise awareness about your business, as well as, develop connections with the community.

The Power Of "Thank You"

This simple tool is often overlooked and forgotten: the power of "thank you". I have seen therapists build successful businesses quickly with this simple tool. After every new customer comes to visit, gift them with a handwritten thank you card sent via the US mail. People who utilize this old-fashioned act of appreciation find their repeat bookings increase. Remember, the strength of your business lies in the number of repeat customers you have on your list.

When is the last time you received a handwritten thank you card in the mail? When is the last time you felt a business really appreciated you? People want to feel good with their purchases. When a client chooses your business, they are investing their time and money on you. They want to feel their choice was worthwhile and appreciated. Give your clients the gift of "thank you". Thank you cards in the mail catch people off guard. They are not expecting a card in the mail from you. It will put a smile on their face.

In addition to sending a handwritten thank you card, you can include a promotion or offer for returning to your business. (Don't forget the expiration date.)

This invitation to return will let your client know you appreciate the fact that they chose you and you want them to pick you again.

Creating Promotional Offers

Create a variety of promotions to attract a variety of consumers. Do not miss marketing opportunities by limiting the type of promotions you offer.

One way to create a variety of promotions is offer different price points. Create packages for a variety of time. The packages that are 30 minutes will obviously cost less than a 90-minute package. This allows you to offer a variety of different prices.

Test out the popularity of different promotions. One business was really surprised when they decided to offer a temporary promotion for face / neck / shoulder treatment.

They created a 45-minute package that included a face massage, scalp treatment, and neck and shoulders' massage. This package became instantly popular. They discovered many people wanted to experience a pampering session, but the idea of getting undressed with a stranger prevented them for scheduling a 60 or 90-minute full body massage. In addition, they heard positive feedback about how some customers just love their face and scalp touched.

The other reason this package become popular is because of the price. With the shorter sessions, they could offer lower price points. This allows people to enjoy a spa treatment while staying within their budgets.

Another business I worked with, was shocked to attract customers who wanted to experience royal VIP treatment. This business owner created a package called The Royal Treatment. We designed a 2-hour package full of everything decedent and attached a high-end price tag. She was shocked when she started booking this package. She discovered, potential customers celebrating an occasion wanted the royal treatment. Alongside these celebration consumers, she booked the VIP packages with travelers, people on vacation looking for a decedent experience. Offering a variety of packages allowed her to attract different types of consumers.

One way to grow your business is to offer a variety of different promotions and services.

You never know what is possible unless you are willing to present more choices.

Promotions are a wonderful tool to grow your business. Promotions do not mean you under sell. One mistake I have seen many businesses make, is offering too many discounts. A typical mistake I see is they have one service on their menu; massage. The same service for new customers, repeat customers, wellness customers and so forth. They made the mistake of not creating a diverse menu and the mistake of continually offering sale prices. Each week they have limited appointments booked, they get nervous and send out an email blast. They send out emails to same group week after week offering discounted prices.

If you consistently send out emails or offer social media discounts to same group of customers, you train your customers to know you always offer discounts. You train them never to pay regular prices because you always have a special, and that is sure to boomerang on your business.

The best way to create special offers is to use the all-important expiration date. If you are going to offer a special value to the package or drop the price, then use the power of expiration date. This will encourage clients to come in.

Market to different platforms. If you have email lists, text lists and social media followers, rotate the offers. You can still post on all your platforms but post with fun massage facts, massage humor jokes or inspirational posts. You do not want every time you engage with clients to be about discounted offers.

Get creative with your packages. For example, offer a 30-minute session to relax on the massage table before or after treatment. Offer a guided meditation or visualization exercise before the session starts. Offer a soothing beverage and snack. Promotion can include a variety of upgrades. Promotions do not have to mean low prices. Get creative.

Last Minute Deals

On your release form paperwork, you can ask clients if they want to on your last-minute deal list. You can also have a sign-up form at the front desk.

This is a sample of what you can write on the form.

LAST MINUTE DEAL

Would you like to receive our last-minute deals?

If we have an unexpected slow day, we will contact you via email, text or telephone. Your Choice.

If you are free, you can schedule a last-minute appointment at a discounted price. If you are busy, please disregard the voice mail or email. One or less contact a month.

Name _____   E-mail _____   Telephone _____

If you are busy now and you do not want to use this strategy, you may still want to gather information for use on a rainy day.

One great way to utilize this list is when someone new starts to work for you, you can have the new person invest their time in contacting these last-minute clients.

For example, Mary is your new hire.

Mary can call these clients or email them and say something like:

Hello _____,

My name is Mary from _____ (your business name). I am offering a last-minute massage deal. If you are free anytime Tuesday or Wednesday this week, (say dates) you can enjoy a 60-minute massage (state whatever your massage deal is) for only _____ (tell price). This last-minute deal offer is good only with me, Mary. If you would like to schedule, please call back (give number) or go online to (provide link) to book your appointment. Thank you.

I suggest you only contact clients on your last-minute deal who have not been to your business in the past 3 months or longer. Use your last-minute list to get previous inactive clients to return.

Loyalty Reward Program

One way to let your customers know you appreciate them is a loyalty reward program.

This is also smart marketing. The reason this is smart marketing is because customers have many choices. There are many businesses available providing massage therapy services. Help your customers give you their loyalty by rewarding them!

You can create different loyalty programs depending on how busy you are or how fast you want to grow your business. If you are not busy, I would suggest you create a reward as soon as possible.

An offer like: Get 3 massages and receive free 30-minute upgrade on your 4th appointment. This allows you to make money on the 4th session. Customer will get a 90 minute for the price of 60 minute.

Getting a reward on 4th appointment encourages clients to stick with your business.

Another idea is to offer a temporary reward. Let's say, you are just starting and you have more time than dollars to advertising, you may offer a 3-month reward.

Get 3 massages and 4th massage is FREE! - Promotion offer is only available for next 90 days. All appointments must be schedule in the 90-day window.

This will encourage clients to book their appointments soon. You can let them know your regular reward is a 30-minute upgrade but you are offering a special promo for the summer (or whatever season you are in).

If you have many clients and your schedule is consistently full, you can still offer a reward to your clients. In this situation, you might want to offer a free massage therapy enhancement upgrade on the 4th appointment. You can create a list of upgrades available to select from. This will give your client a reward, without you investing more time.

People like to be acknowledged for being a regular client.

A loyalty reward helps you show appreciation and motivates your clients to continue to choose you!

Promotional Referral

Are you legally permitted to offer a referral? Check with your state to see if your type of business is able to offer a referral. In some states, massage therapy is considered medical treatment and a referral would be considered a kick back and against the law.

I suggest two types of referrals. The first is your regular referral policy and the other is a promotional referral. A promotional referral is a great tool to use when your business is slow or you are adding staff and wanting to build their business quickly.

The bigger the promotional referral the more results you will receive. Now, the question is, "what is a referral?" A referral occurs when someone recommends your business to others. You are rewarding the person (the referrer) who is doing your marketing and advertising for you.

Promotional Referral Ideas.

30 Day Promotional Referral

$20.00 store credit for each person they refer who comes to your business in next 30 days.

Encourage your clients to go hustle for you. If you know 3 people who enjoy bodywork, you will have a $60 store credit. This is suggestive sales. You plant the idea that if they get 3 of their contacts to come in, they receive a $60 store credit. Having a $60 stores credit is more of an incentive to share the good news of your business than a $20.00 store credit.

Have a promotional business cards for those new customers. It will be easy for your clients to sell your services to their friends if you are offering them a special package. New customer packages are great.

If you usually sell 60 or 90-minute packages, it can be smart to offer new customer packages with different lengths of time, say, 50 or 80 minutes. You would create a specific name for this package. This allows you to know when your new clients have heard about your new customer offer or if they would be regular paying customers. When a customer calls, you are not sure if they are from a referral or they found your business from your paid advertising campaigns. If they do not ask about new customer packages, then book them a regular price service.

Create new customer business cards and pass out to your clients when you are asking for referrals. This way you can code them or write down the person's name to make sure they get the store credit.

Regular referrals program.

This is your basic referral program. This can be $5.00 to $10.00 store credit. This can be a free enhancement add on. This can be a complimentary 15-minute upgrade.

Again, remember that the bigger the reward the more of an incentive a client will feel inclined to share.

One client I worked with offered a free 50-minute massage for each referral. People thought it was a bad idea, but it was brilliant marketing. This person never invested one penny in marketing. She let her clients do all the marketing for her. Her clients loved referring her and they appreciated their free sessions. How often have you heard of a therapist who tries to offer free chair massage or free massage because they are hoping to build their business? This therapist only invested her time in a free message, after she received a paying customer.

Plus, she tapped into the most powerful way to grow her business; getting new clients from genuine word-of-mouth referrals.

Important: When you get a new customer from referral, contact the customer who did the referral. E-mail, telephone or mail them a thank you.

You want to acknowledge the person who took the time to recommend you! Let them know you appreciate their recommending you. Remind them they have a reward waiting for them on their next visit.

Rebooking Offers

One way to get your schedule full is to get your clients to rebook. Some therapists are uncomfortable asking their customers to rebook. They feel they are being pushy; therefore, they avoid the rebooking opportunity.

One way to offer rebooking is with the soft sale approach. This approach is perfect strategy for any type of personality.

You can help your customers become aware you have a return offer by telling them. Your clients may not be aware of your rebooking policy. Sharing the information is one way you contribute to them.

You can let them know of your policy in a way that feels comfortable. One way is to have printed material with information about your rebooking policy. A business card with your re-booking prices is an excellent tool. You may offer a return-in 30-days program with a price list attached. You can hand each client that business card, and let them know if they return within 30 days, they will qualify for this wellness price. This is a soft sale technique. It brings awareness, but, it does not require an instant response.

Another idea for showcasing your rebooking plan is to have a picture frame with a $10.00 bill (or whatever amount you want) inside the frame. Tape a crisp $10.00 bill to piece of paper and type words

Re-Book In 24 Hours for $10.00 Off.

You can point to the picture frame. Share with your customer, if they book their next appointment in the next 24-hour window, they will receive $10.00 off. This allows the client to rebook immediately. Several businesses I work with have been surprised by how many appointments they rebook with this simple, suggestive sales technique.

Clients have told them they really value the rebooking offer as it helps them get their next appointment locked into their schedule. Many clients tell them if they do not schedule their next massage appointment and locked it in their calendar, they end up waiting too long for their next massage. If they wait too long between appointments, their body suffers the side effects. This has helped many therapists realize, suggesting rebooking is really a contribution to their clients.

Thanks, But No Thanks

Sometimes the best thing you can do for your business is turn away business. This may come as a shock to some of you. In our society, there is the age-old cliché that the "customer is always right". I do not believe this. I believe that we all have the freedom to choose.

Clients get to decide if they want to try your services, and they get the freedom to decide if they want to return to your business.

I believe businesses have that same choice.

Occasionally, a customer will come to your business and will not be a match to you. It is ok for you to say, thanks, but no thanks. I know many stories of therapists who try to work with challenging or difficult customers. They feel obligated. They exert so much energy trying to satisfy a customer who is not a match. If you find yourself dealing with a customer who is demeaning, a bully or just someone uncomfortable to work with, give yourself permission to say "no, thank you".

I find people feel empowered when they set boundaries and expectations for themselves. You come to the table being professional and respectful, and you deserve the same

I heard motivational speaker, Tony Robbins, share a similar experience. His seminars sell out to hundreds and thousands of people. He said occasionally, there are one or two people who are impossible to please. They come to the table looking to argue or create conflict. Tony shared his team offers that type of customer a full refund and tells them "No, thanks. We are not a match".

Your peace of mind, and your state of happiness is important. Never compromise that. Businesses who honor themselves and their staff feel happier and feel more comfortable at work. The job satisfaction reflects in their performance and in their attitude. You deserve to feel your best. You deserve to achieve your dreams and arrive at your destination. It is my hope the tools from this book can help make your journey more comfortable as well as help you enjoy the ride.

Massage Therapy Enhancements

Benefits and Descriptions of Popular Massage & Spa Add Ons

Book 6

Introduction

Massage therapy is a powerful tool for health and wellness. More and more people are becoming aware of the benefits of massage. Massage feels great and is good for you.

This book is going to explore a variety of massage tools that enhance your massage experience. Discover the benefits of different massage modalities. Sample different types of massage and find new favorites.

Massage therapy has a variety of styles, techniques and types of services. Step outside your typical routine. Try a different massage style or add on a new massage therapy enhancement.

When we are hungry it is nice to have a variety of flavors and options. It is comforting to have our regular dishes, yet sometimes we want to try something new. It is always a pleasant surprise when we try something new and we discover a new favorite.

Some days when we dine out we are in mood for something light and refreshing, other times we might be craving something more fulfilling. At times, we want comfort food. Food can satisfy many moods and needs.

Massage therapy can be like dining. The menu can offer a variety of items. Depending on your mood and what is going on with your body, you can customize your massage session to meet your needs and wants.

Massage customers and massage businesses enjoy the benefits of different massage therapy enhancements and massage tools.

If you are non-professional at home massage giver and you want to explore some new massage tools and techniques, this book will give you insights and ideas. You will, also, learn the benefits of different massage therapies.

If you are a business owner and you want to add on massage enhancements or offer a variety of massage packages this book is a perfect tool.

Some of the therapies have been around for years, and some of the tools are new innovations. There is something for all types of consumers.

Dive into the huge pool of massage therapy options. Discover tools that help with specific issues. Find new favorites. Take your massage experience to the next level with massage therapy enhancements!

Basalt Hot Stone Massage

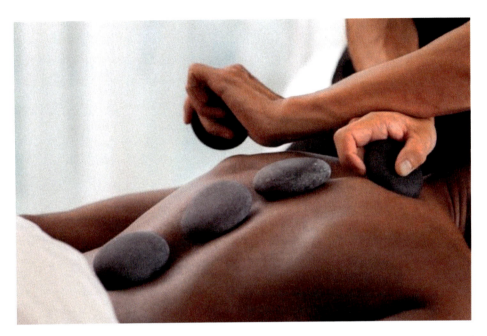

The daily stress of life makes one vulnerable to various aches and pains, mental and physical. Massage offers an effective, safe and enriching way to cope. If seeking massage, then what better way to soak in complete relaxation than by having a basalt hot stone massage. The basalt stones are formed from volcanic eruptions and found near coastal regions. It is suitable for a hot massage because its content of magnetic iron which holds heat. It is rich in iron and magnesium, and an admixture of oxygen and silica. The appropriate size is chosen and prior to its use the stones are heated.

The many advantages of basalt hot stone massage are:

- It generates a complete relaxation experience and soothes the tensed and tight muscles. It induces a calming effect on the body. With relaxed muscles the therapist can massage the deeper tissues and aid in releasing tension.

- Because of the presence of magnetic iron in the basalt stone, it is capable of holding heat for prolonged period of time. The massage in the particular area helps in improving the blood and lymphatic circulation. A perfect circulation makes one liberated from weariness of mind and body.

- It is a safe and gentle way to alleviate pain resulting from arthritis. It loosens up stiff joints and takes care of various aches and pains in the body resulting from a hectic lifestyle.

- The heat generated by the stone uplifts the massage experience. It has higher penetrating powers that achieve relaxation of the mind. Thus, it aids in inducing a sound sleep.

- Evolved over 4000 years and an ancient practice used in many cultures like native Americans, ancient Romans and Egyptians; its charm of providing a deep relaxing experience in spas is truly mesmerizing.

This massage is for clients who seek deeper tissue massage. The massage helps in having a calming effect on the central nervous system.

Bamboo Massage

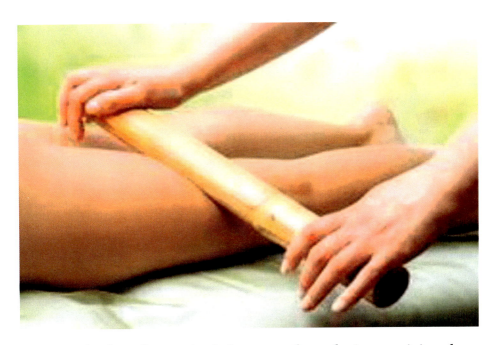

Look no further if your tired tissues seek a relaxing, reviving deep tissue massage, Bamboo massage is just for you. Bamboo massage is unique in its way as it involves Swedish or deep tissue massage using the heated bamboo.

Bamboo has always been regarded as a symbol of strength, resilience, youth, fertility and youth; it is no wonder that it has gained a definitive place in the beauty industry.

The amazing benefits of bamboo massage evolve from the wonderful technique of heating the bamboo sticks and applying on the body by rolling or kneading.

To provide impactful deep tissue massage, bamboo stalks of different sizes and dimensions are heated and applied to the body with the aid of massage lotion and strong pressure.

The heat involved in the technique (Pyroelectricity) and (Piezoelectricity) pressure applied together generate an energetic charge which lead to relaxing soothing effects.

Bamboo massage is rapidly gaining popularity as an effective tool to alleviate modern-day stress and generate natural, safe and effective relief from various physical and emotional problems.

The benefits of Bamboo massage are profound:

Faster relief in pain.

It enhances joints and muscles flexibility.

Efficiently takes care of the spasms, aches and tensions in the body.

Provides instant and lasting relief.

Enhances vitality and causes spurge of energy.

Helps in toning of the body by getting rid of the cellulite.

Rejuvenates and re energises the fatigue tissues post exercise and boosts endurance.

Enhances the tone and texture of the skin. Bamboo extract contains silica that assists the body to absorb essential minerals such as potassium, calcium and magnesium. Silica is known to revitalize the skin and hair.

Provides destressing effects and induces natural sound sleep.

It causes the release of endorphins that are known as the body's natural pain killers.

Jade Roller Face Massage

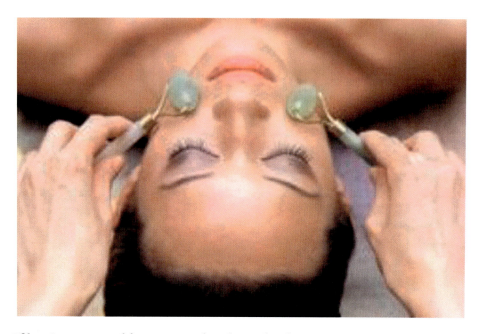

If lasting natural beauty and radiant look are on your agenda, then jade roller face massage should be on your list. Though it may sound new, it is no novice in the field of beauty. Jade, a crystal has been regarded as a mark of grace, beauty and longevity in Chinese culture since as long as 7th century. They are thought to have healing and protective properties.

The jade roller is designed as a handheld massager with two jade stones fixed at the two ends. When it is used in conjunction with other skin care products such as lotions, serums and oils, it helps their deeper penetration into the skin. The roller conveniently can be rolled into delicate parts of the face like eyes, neck and around the mouth. When associated with the skin, it gives a refreshing feeling.

The many amazing advantages of jade roller face massage are:

*Improves blood circulation and diminishes the swelling.

*Reduces the appearance of fine lines and wrinkles by increased circulation.

*Takes care of the dark under-eye circles and gets rid of puffiness due to weariness.

*It activates the lymphatic system and in turn aids with the lymphatic drainage, and markedly reduces the inflammation in the face as a result of stagnation of the lymphatic system.

*Improves the skin complexion and lends a natural glow.

*Boosts the elasticity of the skin.

Hailing from the 7th century in China, the jade roller face massage has found a unique and special place in the modern-day spas.

Himalayan Salt Stone Massage Therapy

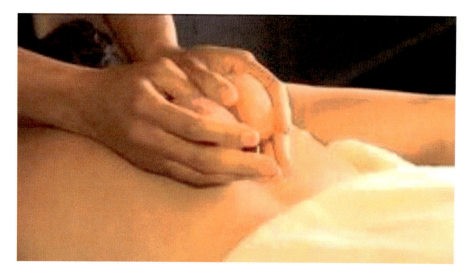

Himalaya, the abode of light, the epitome of serenity and the remedy to every quest. Can anything derived from it be ordinary? Himalayan salt stone is meticulously picked from the base of the Himalayan mountains and was a part of the primal sea long ago prior to when the geologic forces created one of the world's highest peaks.

It is proved beyond doubt that Himalayan salt stone is the purest and the most useful salt ever used for massage.

Originated from the primal sea, the Himalayan salt stone is packed with 84 naturally occurring minerals and elements. The massage with Himalayan Salt Stone explores its variety of divine benefits on the human mind and body. The salts may to be used hot or cold. The advantages are much above than the traditional hot stone massage making use of basalt stones.

Himalayan Salt Stone Massage benefits:

During a hot Himalayan Salt Stone massage, negative ions are generated from the exposure to heat and generates a unique feeling of inner peace, tranquility and mental repose.

The heat generated from Himalayan salt aids in improving the blood circulation, relaxing the deeper tissues of the body, soothes the sore muscles and relieves the stiffness in the joints.

There is no better way to pamper the skin with so subtle, pure moisturizers present in the Salt Stones. The skin regains its lost youth and sublimes with a natural glow. Gently exfoliating the skin and the 84 minerals aid in revitalizing skin making it retain its lost glow.

Acts as a detoxifier.

Induces natural sound sleep, invariably acting as a genuine stress booster.

The Himalayan stones are also effective anti micro- bacterial salts.

Let your body and mind sink into a Himalayan salt stone massage, a unique, wholesome healing technique that grounds and balances the body's electromagnetic field, central nervous system and meridians. Indulge your weary body into a gentle relaxing massage that sets you free of stress, environmental pollutions and creates harmony and alignment of mind, body and spirit. Submerge into the Himalayan salt stone massage and experience rejuvenation and re-energizing moments.

MASSAGE CUPPING

As innovative as the name sounds, massage cupping. Its use for health reasons has been documented in oldest medical textbooks in the world, the Ebbers Papyrus, in 1,550 BC. It has been practiced as a healing method in Egyptian, Chinese, and Middle Eastern cultures since ages.

Unlike the regular massage therapy, cupping massage the inverse method is followed. Here no pressure is applied to the skin, rather the skin is sucked in or raised into the cup. This process of suction of the skin to tug the skin, tissues and even the muscles is known as cupping. This cupping is achieved by placing cups made up of glass, bamboo, earthenware, silicone or plastic on the skin.

The skin is sucked in because of the vacuum that is created. There has been evolution is the techniques of cupping over a period of years, however the basic principle remains the same.

As a result of suction, there is transient discoloration of the skin – red, blue or purple. This is evident more strikingly if there is an injury or blocked energy at the place where cupping was carried out.

This alternative healing method is non-invasive, inexpensive, effective yet safe and can be performed in conjunction with many types of treatments. Cupping massage has various health benefits.

Due to the process of suction created by the cup, there is resultant improved circulation and subsequent pain relief. It aids in removing the toxins from the body tissues.

Cupping is usually performed on the soft, muscular areas of the body, like back or thighs. Depending on the comfort of the client, the cups are moved or kept fixed at a place – moving cupping or fixed cupping.

Cupping is an excellent way to ease pain, inflammation, enhance blood flow, generate mental and physical well-being and provides relaxation to the deep tissues and the mind.

Kansa Wand

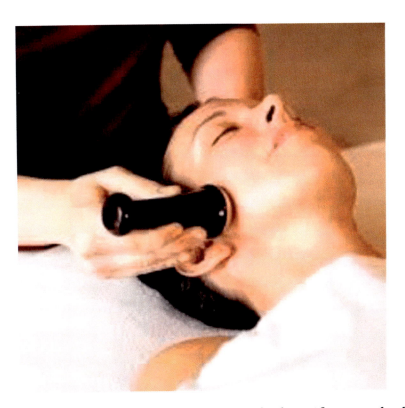

The Kansa Wand face massage suits you the best if you are looking for a gentle face-lifting therapy that also nourishes and rejuvenates the weary tissues of the face, shoulder and the neck.

The massage incorporates the use of a bronze-capped wand called Kansa and is a perfect amalgam of metals (tin and copper) as advocated by Ayurveda, the most ancient holistic traditional healing.

With the help of the essential oils such as jojoba oil the wooden hand handle (Kansa Wand) is gently moved over the face, shoulder and neck region using circular strokes around the eyes, cheeks and jaw.

For a thorough, revitalizing experience the shoulders and neck are also massaged. The massage lets one soak into the warm, serene and relaxing arena. It provides a reenergizing feeling for the mind, body and the spirit. The Kansa wand by the way of soothing friction aids in pulling acidity from the tissues.

The wonderful benefits of Kansa Wand massage include:

Alleviates the pain in shoulder, face, neck and back muscles, leaving one refreshed and relaxed.

Tenderly lifts the facial skin and rejuvenates the deeper tissues.

Acts as a detoxifier, eliminates the acidity and establishes harmony in body, mind and spirit.

Free yourself from electronic gadget, chemicals and harmful radiations; it is the perfect way to indulge in a holistic therapy that creates a positive impact on the energies of the body, via the meridians & chakras, reinstalls balance and harmony in all the systems of the body.

MASSAGE BLADING

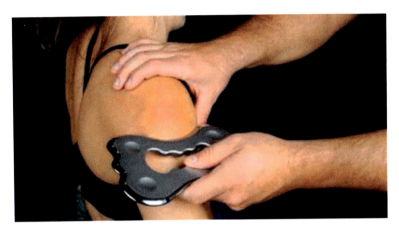

'Blading', the word sounds like a weapon, it is far more beneficial when used in context of a massage technique. The technique involved is called Graston Technique where the soft tissues of the body such as muscles and fasciae are soothed by instrument-assisted mobilization.

A unique massage technique, it constitutes of a maneuver where the skin is gently scraped. The intention of this special therapy is to spot the areas of restriction to motion and release the scar tissue.

Candidates who can get immense relief from massage blading include athletes or sports people who have suffered muscle injuries, have chronic hip pain or limb pains. People active in swimming or indulging in overhead lifting can suffer from chronic shoulder pain and blading can help them ease the pain and restore the movement pain free.

Physically active people who have muscle cramps and pains in the body owing to excessive exercise can seek a safe relief from blading.

People with muscle pains who would not like to or cannot use oral pain killers like NSAIDs can gain good relief from blading.

Massage blading has many benefits. The main goal of this therapy is to alleviate the patient's pain and enhance the function.

The therapy works on the scar tissue occurred as a result of muscle trauma or a pulled ligament, tendon or fascia and gently break them down so as to offer a comfortable, pain free range of motion.

It eliminates fascia restriction offers unhindered range of motion.

It brings down the restrictions towards movements by stretching the connective tissue and aligns the concerned soft tissue structure such as muscle, fascia, tendons or ligaments.

REFERENCES

The Graston Technique: An Instrument Assisted Soft Tissue Manual Therapy For Back Pain, The Graston Technique. Retrieved from https://www.spine-health.com

Marble Cold Stone Massage

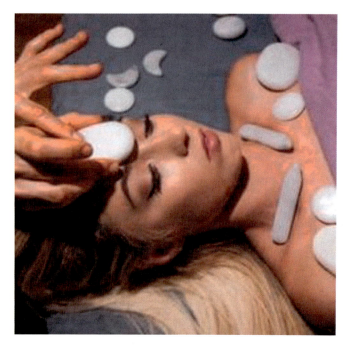

A massage is not just a feeling of the skin being rubbed, but an uplifting experience that soothes the mind, body and the soul. The use of stones during massage has been followed since ages. Stones are the form most closest to the nature, it aids in releasing pains from various parts of the body and also stimulates the different pressure points located in the body.

What better to rejuvenate and recharge the body and mind than to indulge in a cold stone massage using marble stones.

The are many reasons to use marble. Marble is 11 degree Fahrenheit cooler as compared to any other stone in nature, its ability to hold cold and absorb heat is remarkable.

Benefits of marble cold stone massage:

The therapeutic advantages consist of enhanced blood circulation, easing of pain, alleviation of swelling and inflammation, boosting of the body's metabolism and reduction of tension. It improves the muscle tone and enhances body's stimulation.

Acts as a potent decongestant, that aids in the removal of the wastes and toxins from an inflamed tissue, diminish the swelling and establishes proper blood flow.

When applied on the face, it helps to reduce the puffiness and dark circles and effectively enhances the skin tone. It eliminates the pain and relive the congestion caused by the blocked sinuses.

It promises good results in menstrual pain when placed on the abdomen by pulling swelling away from the uterus and thus reduces the menstrual discomfort.

Beneficial to athletes who have sustained trauma. The massage helps in reducing the pain and swelling in the affected tissues and muscles and fastens the healing process.

The cold stone massage has a refreshing effect on the client who prefer cold rather than heat. It aids in lowering the blood pressure. It surely does boost one's mood and uplifts the energy levels.

Hot Stone Foot Massage

There is no station beyond the hot stone foot massage, for it's the ultimate in relaxing and revitalising the weary tired feet and we assure you we will leave no 'stone' unturned to make you smile.

The modality of incorporating hot stones as a tool into the eastern and modern massage techniques generates a unique experience of relaxation for the mind and the body.

This massage has become the need of the hour because of its miraculous therapeutic capability to eliminate the stress and tensions in the body and mind we face routinely. Massage is the safest, non- medicinal, non- invasive yet effective way to rejuvenate.

The stones are used as an aid to make the entire experience much more soothing and relaxing. The stones used are lightweight and smooth in texture and it enhances the experience and the advantages of the massage.

The hot stones are formed from basalt and is rich in iron which attributes it the quality of retaining the heat. The stones help the therapist to relax the deep muscles and still be gentle and less painful as compared to deep tissue massage. the particular massage offers the muscles of the feet to relax in their natural resting position thus allowing less pain and better flexibility in that area.

Hot stone foot massage generates the following benefits:

Relieves and relaxes the tired aching foot muscles.

Takes care of the swelling

Alleviates the leg cramps

Improves blood circulation and relieves tension.

Gets rid of the toxins from the body.

The hot stones help in elevating the experience of the massage

An apt tool to restore balance

Dry Brushing

Stay young not just at heart but also at skin. Aging is an inevitable fact of life but looking your age can be evitable. A good skin regime consists of good sleep, lots of water, nutritious food and appropriate skin care.

For we all agree that the best cosmetic is a great looking skin with a healthy glow. And beautiful skin requires a meticulous skin regime. This article about dry brushing aims to glorify the various therapeutic and cosmetic benefits. The skin performs the function of cooling the body on a hot day, eliminates the toxins, absorbs vitamin D and also acts as an effective barrier preventing the entry of various bacteria that surround us.

Dry brushing involves soft, gentle strokes with an appropriate brush starting from the feet and going towards the center of the body.

Dry brushing is an invaluable tool to brush off the dead cells and facilitates waste removal through the lymph nodes. It stimulates the lymphatic system, thus comes across as an efficient detoxification tool.

It gently exfoliates the skin leading to removal of the dead cells, enhances the appearance, facilitates easy breathing of the skin by opening up the clogged pores.

It enhances the blood circulation of the skin and helps adequate removal of the metabolic waste.

It helps in getting rid of cellulite. The technique of dry skin brushing leads to softening of the hard-fat deposits below the skin and arranges the fat deposits more uniformly creating to reduce the appearance of cellulite.

Dry brushing aids in reducing cellulite by eliminating toxins responsible for the break down connective tissue.

SUGAR SCRUBS

Sugar being a natural humectant attracts moisture from the atmosphere into the skin. Thus, a sugar scrub not only exfoliates the skin, but also at the same time they actually help hydrate your skin and help retain moisture inside. Hence the skin does not feel dry post scrub.

Sugar is a natural source of glycolic acid which is an alpha hydroxy acid (AHA) which goes deep in the skin and separates the bonded skin cells which enhances cell turnover which leads to fresher, younger-looking skin. Glycolic acid cats as a soothing agent for a sun-damaged and aging skin.

 As compared to salt scrub, sugar scrub has more advantages such as the latter is gentler than salt. Salt scrub can lead to microscopic tears in the skin and can strip the skin of its essential oils which a sugar scrub does not. Sugar being available in small particles form an important ingredient of body scrubs.

It acts as an excellent topical exfoliant by removing dead surface skin cells and unveils the glowing, healthy-looking skin underneath.

Sugar scrub is effective enough to be used twice a week only. It is a delightful experience for the skin when carried out in winter as removing the top dead layer of the skin aids moisturizers seep in more deeply and hydrate longer. Sugar scrub can be used throughout the year for a glowing radiant looking skin which is adequately moisturized.

Brown sugar scrubs are very gentle and free of abrasive effect and can be even used by those with sensitive skin. People suffering from psoriasis and eczema can also used sugar scrub and it enhances the healing process of the skin.

THAI HERBAL MASSAGE BALLS

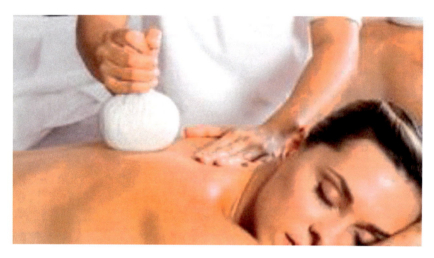

Thai herbal heat massage balls have been used since ages as an effective way to soothe sore muscles of war-fatigued soldiers during the Thai-Burmese battles in the Ayutthaya period.

The major components in the Thai herbal ball may differ from place to place and also based on the ailments of the client. However, the main ingredients of the Thai herbal balls are: Plai (Thai ginger), Kaffir Lime, Turmeric, Acacia leaves, Menthol, Camphor, and Myrtle Grass.

Thai herbal ball is applied post massage. The process includes relaxing the aching muscles and stiff joints by appropriate stretching and compression manoeuvres of Thai massage. Thereafter, the heated herbal compress is applied over majority of the body. The herbal ball rubbed over the skin in a rolling fashion is rolled applying gentle pressure and circled right on the body.

Since the herbal balls are directly rolled over the skin, a warm sheet can be used for privacy and to prevent the escape of the heat from the Thai herbal balls.

The numerous benefits of Thai Herbal Balls massage are:

*It induces profound relaxation, eliminates stress and fatigue, enhances emotional and physical well-being.

*It soothes aching and sore muscles and reduces the stiffness in the joints. The hot compress provides wonder relief from pain of arthritis and migraines. The massage helps in replenishing the lost vigor and stamina.

*It aids in inducing a calming and invigorating effect on the mind and body, thus is highly beneficial in chronic stress and anxiety.

*It enhances the blood and lymph circulation and stimulates the internal organs. It cleans and heals the skin by facilitating cell growth.

*The potent herbs present in the compress have unique anti-inflammatory, antiseptic, astringent and antioxidant properties. They are recommended in upper in causing comfort in upper respiratory problems such as asthma, common cold and bronchitis. The Camphor and menthol present in the herbal balls facilitate the breathing.

Sabrina Tonneson

Non-Professionals - At Home Massage Tips

If you are a massage fan and want to begin a home massage routine here are a few tips to help you get more for your massage experience. If you are exchanging massages with a friend or partner the most important thing to do is communicate. Find out what muscles groups and areas are your partner's favorite. Often people receiving the message do not want to share what they like and dislike.

Take some time before the exchange to write a list of your favorite areas. When doing the exchange, if your partner is doing a technique that you love, tell them. The more information the giver has, the better then massage will be for the receiver.

If you are going to invest your time giving a massage, why not give the best massage you can. Each body is different and each person has different ideas on what they consider to be the best massage. Be mindful of their preferences. You want to customize each massage for the receiver.

Next set up the atmosphere. Create an atmosphere that allows the mind to relax. Soothing sounds can slow down a mind filled with to do lists or anxious thoughts. Scents can help the body and mind to relax. Pick your favorite scents and do some deep breathing before your routine starts. The giver can remind you before each session to take in 10 deep breaths. During your session, if you remember, do more deep breathing.

Darken the room for mental quietness. The mind tends to slow down and release stress in dark. If you cannot darken the room cover the eyes with a warm towel or eye pillow.

Some people talk during the massage exchange. If you want to gain more benefit from your massage, try to receive in silence. The reason this is valuable is because the mind stays active during conversation, even if the conversation is light. The mind has to stay alert in order to participate in the conversation. When the mind is given permission to be quiet, it will begin to turn off so to speak. The more relaxed you are mentally, the more your body will relax physically.

Giving the massage in silence tends to be boring for the giver. When the giver is bored, the giver may want to cut the time short or not want to exchange massages often. Create a way for the giver to enjoy their time. One way the giver can enjoy giving is to get mentally distracted in a movie, tv episode or audio book. You can use headphones. If the receiver does not mind background sound, you can listen to your movies or shows on a low volume.

If the giver is distracted and entertained mentally, the hands-on massage time will fly by. In the beginning you might need to concentrate more on the massage technique, but with practice, you will quickly find a rhythm and discover you can give a quality massage on autopilot.

If you are going to try services in this book, there are many ways to buy the products and free ways to learn techniques. I suggest you google the products you want to try. You will find a range of prices. I have found some products are more affordable on

Amazon or Ebay. Massage Warehouse and other massage supply stores will carry the products.

Crock pots from big box stores like Walmart are more affordable than hot stone heaters at massage supply stores.

If you are going to buy a massage table, check out craigslist. The massage industry has a very high turnover rate. Many massage therapists quit and sell like new massage equipment on craigslist for very low prices.

Learning basic massage and massage therapy enhancements can be found free online. YouTube is an excellent resource. Many therapists offer free training videos on YouTube. Contact massage schools for workshops. Many massage school offer workshops to the public. Instructional DVD's is another resource to learn massage techniques. Google the technique you want to learn and discover a variety of options.

Many non-professionals develop wonderful skills and build an awesome collection of massage tools. Learning massage for personal use is a valuable life time skill.

Remember, take a few minutes before the massage exchange to create a relaxing atmosphere, communicate your wants and set up any necessary equipment. Do the prep work before your massage exchange, in order to get the most out of the experience.

The easier you make it to give, the more often you will want to exchange and reap the benefits of massage.

Professionals - Tips

This book can be a great benefit for your massage business. One way to use this book to build your business and attract new clients is by educating your clients and potential clients the benefits of different massage therapy enhancements.

Use images and description to promote different services on your social media and your newsletters.

A picture is worth a thousand words. Use images of the massage tools you are promoting or the massage techniques you want to highlight.

You can display the images on your website, your social media and at your office. You can include a bullet point list of the benefits.

Many clients will see the images and their curiosity will be peaked. They will ask you questions about the tools and service. This is a soft way to promote.

Another way to promote these massage therapies is to make a list of the enhancements you want to include in your practice. Have a printed list available for your clients to see. You can design this flyer yourself or hire a graphic designer to create an attractive flyer fo you. Display this flyer at your office. Share it on your website.

This book is a great coffee table book to have in your waiting area. Clients naturally look for things to read or check out as they wait. Clients can read the different therapies and their benefits from this book.

For more information on how to earn more money, without working more hours, check out my book, <u>Add On The Serenity</u>. Create Popular Upgrades That Sell. Work Smart & Make More Money.

www.MassageMarketing101.com

Made in the USA
Columbia, SC
09 December 2021